FROM LACK
TO ABUNDANCE

Re-Engineering Your Mindset

From Lack to Abundance

Dr. Jean C. Dor, DBA

3 ABUNDANCE MINDSET

Published by GAJIJ CAPITAL LLC

GAJIJ LEADERSHIP EDUCATION

Book Cover by Quincy J. Dor

ACKNOWLEDGMENTS

My wife Judeline Dor, friend Jr. Augustin, and staff Juliette Dor, Michemarna Dor, Stephanie Destinville, and sons Jacob Dor and Quincy Dor all helped me to write this book.

I wrote this book in honor of my brother Genson Dor "BLAN".

Rest in peace, my dear friend!

CONTENTS

INTRODUCTION: BEING RICH IS YOUR BIRTHRIGHT 7

1.   DESIRE FOR SUCCESS... 13

2.   DISCOVER YOUR PURPOSE 22

3.   BELIEVING IS SEEING... 45

4.   AS YOU THINK, SO YOU BECOME 51

5.   ABUNDANCE MINDSET 64

6.   EVERYONE HAS THE RIGHT TO WEALTH 72

7.   TAKE ACTION 83

8.   FAILURE IS NOT THE END OF THE WORLD....................... 100

9.   PROVEN SUCCESS METHODS 106

10. THE LAW OF USE 109

11. MAKE THE BEST USE OF YOUR TIME 115

13   CHANGE YOUR DESTINY 136

"While we don't always get what we want, we always get what we choose." –John Maxwell

INTRODUCTION: BEING RICH IS YOUR BIRTHRIGHT

When you look at the world, do you ever wonder why some people are wealthy while others struggle to feed their families? Those who answered yes aren't alone. 60% of Americans live paycheck to paycheck and many can't pay their credit card bills on time because of so much debt. Quite frightening, isn't it? I am not trying to depress you with these facts. I just want to reassure you that you're not alone if you're not rich like you'd like to be. But the good news is that your current financial situation doesn't have to last. It's possible to live a life without stress by not worrying about money. The choice is yours!

It is your birthright to be wealthy!

By reading this book, you will learn how to become financially independent, which will enable you to take control of your future. There are many ways to become wealthy, but most people succeed by following a few universal laws and cultivating a growth mindset. Implementing these universal laws leads to financial freedom.

Financial success, according to Jim Rohn, is living off your own resources. Tony Robbins once said that financial freedom is having everything you need today, plus a few luxuries you wish to have in the future, without having to work for it. At this moment, many thoughts may be swirling through your head. In fact, you might even wonder if being financially successful requires millionaire status. In simple terms, no; however, most people hope to become millionaires someday. Financial success does not require millionaire status, but it can offer many benefits. In the end, financial success depends on how an individual achieves his or her financial goals.

According to Credit Suisse's latest wealth report, 46.8 millionaires exist worldwide. The United States is home to 18.6 million millionaires. Seventy-eight percent of millionaires worked their way up from humble beginnings. A mere 22% of millionaires inherited their wealth from their parents. Why is that important to us? Considering this data, it is safe to say that anybody can become rich by applying the law of riches. Wallace D. Wattles, the author of The Science of Getting Rich, said that wealth isn't dependent on environment, family, talent, or education. If one person can be wealthy, we can all be. All of us were born with the ability to gain wealth, but somewhere along the line, some of us believed we had to become geniuses to become wealthy. This is not the case at all. Thomas Edison, Elon Musk, Steve Jobs, or any other genius we admire did not have brains that were inherently better than yours. Each of them was a normal person like us who changed his or her life for the better. They achieved the impossible despite their lack of special abilities. Because of developing a growth mindset, they could overcome challenges, ultimately leading to success. Despite an initial rejection from his high school's varsity basketball team, Michael Jordan went on to become one of the most celebrated players in history due to his determination. His powerful statement was, "I have missed more than 9000 shots in my career." I've lost almost 300 games. 26 times I've trusted to take the game-winning shot and missed. And that is why I succeed." As you can see, the only way you can lose is if you quit.

DEVELOP A WEALTH MINDSET

If we wish to become wealthy, we must deprogram and reprogram everything we ever learned about money. As James Allen said, "We are where we are in life because of what we have learned; if we dislike the results, we must change them." To get what we never had, we must do what we have never done before. As you strive to accumulate success, you need to become a student and learn from those who have achieved massive financial success. One of the best ways to do that is to learn from those who have gone before us.

> **To get what we never had, we must do what we have never done before.**

Taking the time to study people like Jesus, Andrew Carnegie, Jim Rohn, and Zig Ziglar will lead us to great wisdom that will last a lifetime. Because of their financial wisdom, we may shape ourselves for great wealth in the future.

I think it's crucial to analyze your inner wisdom if you have studied all those people. I just mentioned but have not yet achieved financial success. Find out why you keep failing in your quest to become rich. This will not be a simple task. There will be some soul-searching involved, but the results will be amazing. Once you identify the exact reason (s) behind your failure to become wealthy, you must immediately change your mindset. *Everything starts with the mind*. In the words of one writer, "No achievement is possible without the mind."

> **There are no achievements without the mind.**

Upon discovering a new philosophy through your soul-searching, you need to align your mind with it. Matthew 9:16 warns us against bringing the past into the future: "No one puts a piece of a new garment on an old one." To reap new benefits, we must become new creatures. It was Jesus' understanding that sticking to our old ways and bringing in a new method would be a recipe for failure. Instead, we must change our way of thinking. It is time for the past to be buried! Changing our focus from what we could perceive as a failure to what we can perceive as success will enable us to attract genuine success into our lives. At the end of the day, who we are is determined by what we think about. We store everything we think about in our subconscious, no matter how good or bad it is. Thinking correctly leads to excellent results, whereas thinking incorrectly leads to bad results. If you wish to achieve lasting change, it is essential to adhere to the law of the subconscious mind. Every action we take must be intentional. Choosing to be intentional gives us the power to control the course of our lives. We are no longer at the mercy of friends who are always ready to share their opinion on anything we consider worthwhile.

We have gifted humanity with the greatest gift of all: the power to choose. What we choose is up to us. Whether we remain in making current situation or make better decisions that will change the course of our lives is completely up to us. The path to enriching and improving our wealth ability is more likely to be enriched and improved when we choose to revolutionize our thinking. It's possible for us to take charge of our lives and pave our own way. By making our own decisions, we can create the life we desire without being limited by society's expectations. We have the power to create our own destiny.

WEALTH OBSESSION

Despite what our surroundings and external forces have taught us, we were not born to live average lives. We can be as successful as anyone else in life, but first, we must have the drive to achieve it. According to Napoleon Hill in Think and Grow Rich, desire is the key to wealth. Before we can become rich, we must truly desire it. You cannot be dispassionate about wealth and expect to gain it.

Our desire will be our antidote to all the obstacles we will face as we progress in our quest for riches. Faced with any difficulty, a weak desire will lead us to quit. For us to achieve success as wealthy individuals, we must have a strong burning desire for wealth, as this will enable us to bounce back any time, we fall short. *A righteous person rises despite falling seven times.* It is also essential that we become richly conscious of the idea every single day so that we see ourselves as possessors of it. Some people may visualize themselves in luxury daily to make their dreams of wealth come true. Because of this visualization process, we work toward our goals more effectively and act more quickly. As long as we have perseverance and resilience, we will eventually reach our financial goals.

Wealth must be our driving force and serve as a motivator for our actions. As a result, we will remain motivated and focused on achieving our goals. Putting effort and dedication into our dreams can make them come true. It is important to remember that nothing is impossible and that we can achieve our goals. We can achieve our dreams if we have the right attitude and determination. Keeping a positive attitude and striving for success is essential.

> **Becoming rich is your birthright, no matter what.**

CHAPTER 1

1. DESIRE FOR SUCCESS

Massive success in life begins with the desire to become rich. That's all there is to it. Getting rich won't happen unless you have a mindset that attracts it. The way you approach it makes all the difference. Even though having a good attitude alone cannot guarantee success, having a poor attitude about it will certainly lead to failure. It is likely because of this that two people can work the same job and get paid the same wage, but one becomes rich while the other remains financially unstable. The decision to become rich is only the beginning of a long and challenging journey. Afterward, you must decide to change your mind from one that is poverty conscious to one that is prosperity conscious. Reject any thoughts that do not align with your mindset towards riches as you work to improve it.

As Napoleon Hill notes, achieving success requires becoming success conscious. It is impossible for people to see themselves as failures and think they will succeed. That's not how it works. No matter the outcome, our minds will always gravitate toward our deepest thoughts, regardless of success or failure.

It is important to note that our brain has two essential components: the success mechanism and the failure mechanism. Brian Tracy believes failure functions automatically. This part of our brain follows the path of least resistance without discipline, resulting in failure. A goal often triggers the success mechanism, and once we decide to achieve that goal, we can override that mechanism and possibly alter our lives. Craig Groeschel states our thoughts shape our personalities. When our mind becomes consumed by success, we see success all around us; however, if we want failure, it becomes the only thing that plagues our minds, and we see failure everywhere. For example, if you believe you will fail an upcoming test, you may find

> **The decision to become rich is only the beginning of a long and challenging journey.**

yourself feeling anxious and overwhelmed. This can lead to a self-fulfilling prophecy, as your anxiety and lack of focus can make it more difficult to prepare and perform on the test. This is because our minds are wired to focus on what we believe to be true, whether it is positive or negative. By focusing on negative thoughts, our minds will bring to the surface evidence that supports those thoughts, even if it is not true. This can create a negative feedback loop, leading to feelings of helplessness and anxiety. Ultimately, we handle how we think and how we shape our future. Because we have so much control over our thoughts, we should do everything in our power to protect our minds from negative thoughts. Changing our thinking patterns can open up opportunities for acquiring wealth. It is God's desire for us to live life to the fullest. Jesus says in John 10:10 that He came to give us life and to give it to us abundantly. It may be difficult for people to believe they were born to succeed, but it is the truth. From a retrospective point of view, God created and gave Adam everything in the Garden of Eden. Because of the Creator's intention, Adam and Eve lived fulfilling lives. Irish playwright George Bernard well understood that truth. According to him, being poor was a sin. We sin against God's laws when we reject His truth. The laws of God fulfilled and honor God by guiding men in living fulfilling and honorable lives. We must accept these laws and choose to have a positive attitude to become successful.

Even if we have the right attitude about becoming rich, we must also be very persistent in achieving it. Perseverance and determination enable us to overcome adversity. I once heard about a man who attended a self-development seminar. In the days following the seminar, he called all his friends and told them he would join a gym and improve his appearance. After joining his neighborhood gym, he began attending fitness classes regularly. It did not last long; he quit after just two weeks. He stopped going because he didn't feel like he was making much progress. The health of this man has not improved one bit, and he remains in terrible shape. Even though he sincerely wanted to change his life, his lack of commitment hindered his progress.

PATIENCE IS A VIRTUE

As my grandmother used to say, "Don't rush anything in life. There is no such thing as a coincidence. If it is meant to be, then it will happen." It sounds like good advice, especially since I know God does not give what he has for you to anyone else. We often feel hurried when we compare where others are in life to our own. When comparing ourselves to others, it is difficult to be patient on the road to success. People should consider patience as a valuable quality. Proverbs 21:5 warns us against those who have been hasty in their lives. In the end, it did not satisfy them with the results. According to Solomon, who was probably the richest man in history, "Everyone who is hasty surely comes to poverty." If you are impatient or hasty, you will not enjoy your journey to success. If we asked any wealthy person about their journey, they would say it is the most important aspect. It is on the journey that we grow. When we fail, we learn and turn that failure into a winning strategy. A wise man once said that if you want to achieve your dreams, embrace adversity and embrace failure. A healthy part of getting rich is accepting failure. Fear of failure prevents us from succeeding. Bill Gates faced many failures while starting Microsoft, but he persevered and eventually found success.

THE POWER OF PATIENCE

Nowadays, people want things to happen immediately, which makes practicing patience difficult. Unlike previous generations, they are not used to waiting for things. As a result, many people of this generation are looking for results as soon as they start a new habit. It takes consistency to make new habits lasting and strong because old habits die hard. King Solomon said in Ecclesiastes 7:8: "The end is better than the beginning, and patience is better than pride." Decide today not to rush your goal-achieving process, but practice daily habits. Consistency is key to success: taking small steps every day and being patient with the process. This process is like building a house. It takes commitment and endurance to create a durable structure. The same is true when we form habits: it takes consistent effort to establish them, but the result is a strong, lasting habit.

According to Brian Tracy, success requires three factors. The first step to success is deciding what you want from life. As a second step, you must determine how much you will pay to reach the top. The third step is to resolve to pay that price. As humans, it is in our nature to always do things that come naturally to us. While there is nothing wrong with that, if we are trying to grow, we must venture off the beaten path. Success comes from hard work. It is not a good idea to take the easy road out; it will only lead to ruin, as

Jesus warns his disciples. The road to massive success is narrow and hard, so he advised his disciples to travel through the gate where the road is narrow and hard. If we apply this advice to our lives, regardless of whether we are religious, we can reap substantial rewards. Most people do not think they can succeed on that path, which is why only a few choose to follow that path. It is their failure to develop the advancing mind and the belief that they can become rich that has prevented them from becoming rich. In consequence, their poverty-stricken conditions persist year after year. Despite this, they must change before things change for them. Positive thinking can open up pathways to financial success.

BECOME MORE DILIGENT

Steven Scott, the author of The Richest Man Who Ever Lived, states that we need to be diligent and have a clear vision to achieve true fulfillment. People who cannot be diligent lack understanding, and their efforts often go to waste since they cannot succeed. To tap into our best selves, we must be conscientious. A clear vision, imagination, commitment, and advice-seeking are key to finding fulfillment.

Most people choose not to be diligent in their lives because it is very demanding. Despite the difficulty, the rewards are certainly worth it. It is possible to accomplish incredible things when we are diligent, discover our purpose, and have a clear vision. There is a story in the Bible that is familiar to most people. It appears in Luke 15:11–32. It illustrates how dangerous it is to be hasty and impatient rather than diligent. This is the story of a prodigal son. According to the Bible, a father had two sons, and one of them demanded his inheritance impatiently. After leaving home, the young man traveled abroad and partied until he was bankrupt. With all his money gone, he had to take care of pigs to feed himself. It seemed as if this young man would gladly eat the food pigs ate because he was so hungry. How does this story relate to becoming rich?

It's time to inspect what caused this young man's misfortune. First, he wanted his inheritance before it was due to him. In his impatience, he could not wait for his father to give it to him in time. Because of his decision, he sank to the lowest level of humanity where he craved the food of pigs. The second problem was his lack of self-discipline. Self-discipline is a direct correlation to being successful. You gain self-worth every time you complete your tasks without procrastinating. By doing so, you develop the ability to deal with anything that might impede your progress. You are more likely to become rich if you have high self-esteem. Lack of self-discipline, however, can lead to failure. A lack of self-control causes financial problems, says Brian Tracy. Until we learn to practice self-discipline, we cannot achieve our dreams. When you become a disciplined person, you learn to control your behavior. According to Proverbs 25:28, a man who has no self-discipline is like a city that is left defenseless after being attacked. Doing things for the sake of feeling satisfying a particular passion is not sufficient. We should focus on our goals, use our resources to our advantage, and be mindful of our decisions. Self-discipline is essential to achieve our ambitions and be successful. For instance, when you want to save money, you need to have the self-discipline to track your spending and resist the urge to buy things you don't need.

Do your best to understand how your actions today can affect your future. Tony Robbins once said, "Nothing in life has any meaning except the meaning that you give it. So, make sure that You consciously choose the meaning that is most in alignment with the destiny you've chosen for yourself." As a result, embrace all failures and turn them into excellent opportunities. According to an old saying, people who aren't hasty can delay gratification for a while. They learn to delay the temporary rewards for something much greater in the future. This creates a recipe for financial independence.

> **Embrace all failures and turn them into excellent opportunities.**

People who lack discipline and are hasty will not find solace, no matter how hard they search. They will always depend on those who practice self-control. Keeping yourself disciplined can help you focus on what you want and avoid what you don't want. This self-discipline will make you unstoppable. This is like a marathon runner who continually trains and pushes themselves to the next level; the more they practice, the better they get, and the greater the payoff in the end.

It's never too late to change our lives. If you've been traveling in a direction that has caused you sadness or misery, you can change directions.

> **It is never too late to change our lives.**

By adopting new methods and gaining new wisdom, you can avoid making the same mistakes again. At this point in history, we have access to every opportunity to become rich and successful, but we must decide if that's what we want and if we will work for it. Whether we become rich depends on the choices, we make right now. We must follow through on our resolution once we have made our choice and go confidently toward our dreams.

Hence, now the obvious question is, *how do you become wealthy?* This is a good time to think about what stands between you and earning millions of dollars. It is also important for you to discover what you want to do in life. By doing so, you will strengthen yourself and catapult yourself quickly to the next level. The next chapter will explore how to discover your purpose.

CHAPTER 2

2. DISCOVER YOUR PURPOSE

In order to fully experience life, we were born with various gifts and talents. When we were children, we made those gifts clear to us. As children, most of us knew exactly what we wanted to be when we grew up. However, as we age and the demands of life take over, we forget about our childhood dreams and focus only on surviving. Worry, fear, and intimidation of life's demands cause us to live a lie. That should not be the case, since doubts and fears don't accomplish anything worthwhile. Psalm 139:14 states, "We were fearfully and wonderfully made." God created us lovingly. Thus, to become rich and change the direction of our lives, we have every tool at our disposal.

God gives us the freedom to choose. It makes a world of difference to have that choice. Without discovering our purpose in life and using our superpowers, we will continue to live mediocre lives.

It is tragic to know that 98 people out of every 100 never discover what their true purpose is in life. Regardless of what life throws at them, they simply accept it. As a result, they become slaves to something that they should have already mastered. I believe that is why the Bible mentions God will wipe away every tear from our eyes. As we realize all that we could have been in this life, but never were, I believe we will shed tears after death. On that day, I can imagine the regrets we will have.

As Les Brown once said, "The graveyard is the richest place on earth because it contains all the hopes and dreams that never came true, the books that never came to life, the songs that never came to life, the inventions that never got adopted, the cures that never came to light." It is filled with people who never lived their true purpose. Somewhere along the line, they never sought a reason to do what they did. Success isn't easy, but if you want it, you can achieve it. Our capacity to advance in life directly depends on our ability to accept problems for what they are and take the steps to move forward. In the words of Andrew Carnegie, "Individuals who move towards their goals with a clear and definite purpose are often met with opportunities and assistance from the world around them." This is like building a house; you need the foundation and the right tools to get the desired result. Without a clear vision and hard work, the dream can remain unfulfilled. It's only when we put in the effort that our dreams can become a reality.

> **Define your purpose and develop a logical reason for pursuing it.**

YOUR 'WHY' MATTERS!

Many people don't succeed in life because they don't figure out what their purpose is. In other words, they never discovered why they were here. It is crucial to know why if we want to get rich. By doing so, we can live effectively and efficiently. As Eric Thomas stated in You Owe You, "Walking for your purpose means living up to your full potential and using your gifts every day." But first, we must discover why we are here. It is not by chance that we are here. As part of a well-designed plan, we play an important role. As it says in Romans 8:29, God has plans for those whom he foreknew so that he might be the firstborn among many brothers.

Famous author and writer Mark Twain once said that the two most important days in a person's life are when he or she is born and when they discover why. His assertion suggests that humanity has been seeking to understand why God made them since the beginning of time. Despite this, if we don't know the why, we can't determine where to go and what to do. According to James Allen, "A man must dream of a legitimate purpose in his heart and take steps to achieve that goal." This must originate from the heart." It mirrors what the Bible says, too, "Out of the bounds of the hearts, all good things flow." Those who seek a purpose in life that is meaningful must come from within themselves. It is easy to persist through obstacles when you have a heart-centered purpose since it is something you truly believe in and are passionate about.

25 ABUNDANCE MINDSET

A person who wishes to be wealthy needs to understand that the road to riches is paved with good intentions, but it is only those who are persistent enough who succeed. By embracing problems and persevering through them, they become rich. You may think this is a cliché, especially if you have tried every method available to gain wealth without success. Your belief has caused your failure that getting rich is a matter of environment or education. Perhaps you feel you weren't born lucky, and riches belong to everyone else. Here's the simple truth: you can be rich. Getting rich is possible if Bill Gates does it. Don't be negative, so you don't miss out on valuable facts, laws, and powers that can lead to wealth.

A famous American writer, Wallace Wattles, said that getting rich comes from doing things a Certain Way. I can't think of defeat and achieve success at the same time. Since our minds can only handle one thought at a time, we must think only of prosperity, wealth, good health, and peace. Keep doing, despite temporary failures, by developing the habit of always looking for something more in life. Thomas Edison is said to have tried over ten thousand experiments before developing a successful incandescent lamp. The man did not quit. The only way to win is to keep doing it, even after temporary defeats. For example, Edison once said, "Many of life's failures are people who did not realize how close they were to success when they gave up."

> **The key to success is perseverance to the end.**

People have triumphed over heartbreak and realized their dreams by discovering their motivation. Their success results from learning what it takes to be successful. Jesus' story illustrates that adversity is a part of the journey. Although Jesus lived a sinless life, he had to endure the cross before he could save humanity. Jesus had to endure beating, crucifixion, death, and resurrection before achieving his principal goal. You can succeed if you don't quit, but nothing worth pursuing will come easy.

As the Bible says in Galatians 6:9, "Let us not become weary in doing good, for at the proper time we will reap a harvest if we do not give up." If we do not give up, we will succeed. Today, I want to give you some advice: never give up. Facing difficulties will build resilience. Resilience will help you keep going and eventually reach your goals. With resilience, you can reach success even when the odds are against you. Believe in yourself and never give up! For instance, when facing a tough challenge, draw on your inner strength and don't be afraid to reach out for help. Even if you don't think you can get through it, remember to take each day one step at a time and stay positive.

YOUR PURPOSE MATTERS

The discovery of our purpose in life makes it much easier to contribute positively to society. Despite all the adversities we encounter, it keeps us going. By identifying your purpose, you'll be able to identify what's valuable, and you'll be on your way to achieving it. As Thoreau, an American philosopher, once said, "If one advances confidently toward his dreams and tries to live the life he has imagined, he will meet with a success unexpected in common hours." Defining your purpose and working diligently toward it will make you successful. Before deciding on any endeavor, conduct your due diligence.

Napoleon Hill compared people without purpose to ships without direction. They limit their motivation to what they can see. Worries, fears, troubles, and failures plague them. Purposeful people live a life of faith, hope, and courage because they know they can change their circumstances if they choose to do so. To become one of the top 20%, you need discipline to focus on one task at a time. Let's say that you want to open an insurance agency, but you only have the money to open a documentation preparation business. Focus solely on document preparation business with full faith and confidence that one day it will become an insurance agency. The beauty of giving something your complete attention is that it yields the best results. As a result, we can envision ourselves as already possessing what we truly desire. Motive is the fuel that keeps us focused, and without it, we wouldn't even be able to begin. You should therefore work on what is most important to you until it has reached 100% completion. A multi-track mindset will prevent you from giving each endeavor your full attention and effort if you approach it this way. Some say that those who have developed an ability to keep their minds focused on one particular thing at a time will achieve outstanding success.

Always focus on the prize. It is often said that those who persevere to the end win the race. No matter how many obstacles they face, they make it their mission to finish the race. For example, a marathon runner may experience cramps or other physical pain during the race but keep going until they reach the finish line. They do this because they know that quitting isn't an option. Even when the odds seem insurmountable, they don't give up. Through determination and persistence, they can reach their goals and achieve success.

DETERMINATION AND PERSISTENCE

Once you identify your life's purpose, you will accomplish anything you set out to accomplish. A determination to succeed unlocks all possibilities, so if you want greatness, you must be determined. You can achieve anything you set your mind to. Several years ago, I heard of a man who was terminally ill, and doctors told him he only had six months to live. Instead of focusing on what the doctors said, he focused on walking his daughter down the aisle. A year later, he did just that. He endured the journey because he was determined to live. The key to success is not accepting what others say about you and moving forward with faith.

Thousands of success stories like this exist, but none would have been possible without determination and persistence. Despite missing over 9,000 shots, Michael Jordan became the greatest of all time. People who are determined and persistent are not afraid to try alternative approaches when their previous methods don't work. They remain optimistic and do their best to find the positives in every failure. Despite setbacks, they are confident that every failure can be a learning experience that can lead to increased success in the future. It has been said by Napoleon Hill that "Within every problem or obstacle lies a seed of equal or greater opportunity.". It is your job to find it." You can identify the lesson by focusing on finding solutions to obstacles rather than identifying the cause.

Persistence holds together dreams. If you don't change yourself, nothing will change for you. As you become more persistent in this regard, your dreams will become more achievable. When you are persistent, you will no longer blame others when things don't go as planned. You will instead pick up where you left off and continue to strive for greatness. In our society, those who embrace setbacks are likely to be among the top 20% of successful people. Consistency, hard work, and self-discipline are the keys to success.

To become a millionaire, you must embrace persistence and make it your best friend. There is a story about a young man who wanted to migrate legally to the United States from his native country. Every time he applied for a tourist visa; They denied him. He didn't let that stop him. The sixth time they approved his visa application, he understood that "where there is no struggle, there is no progress." The ability to stay persistent is crucial to reaching the top. Persistence was the most important success principle in the world, according to Calvin Coolidge. There is nothing more common than unsuccessful people with talent, intellect, or education; persistence and determination are everything.

True persistence will enable you to go the extra mile to accomplish your goals. Having the mindset that all obstacles are mental rather than physical will also help you push for more. As Norman Vincent Peale said, "When you

> **If you think of victory over difficulty, you will triumph.**

face a rough situation, know that it is only mental." If you think of victory over difficulty, you will triumph. Because you perceive the problem as rough, it seems rough to you. Reframe the problem because you have the power to overcome it.

LACK OF PERSISTENCE

The lives of people who lack purpose, determination, and persistence are average. Simply put, they are not strong enough to fight. In the words of successful people, they are great starters, but poor finishers. After starting something, they get excited, but quickly give up when it doesn't go as planned. According to Edmund Hillary, an explorer and philanthropist, skills are worthless without persistence. Bob Proctor said that persistent people don't give up. Regardless of what they do, the going will be tough for everyone, but they must continue forward. There is no point in quitting since quitters achieve nothing. They must do everything in their power to succeed. As Dexter Yager said, "If the dream is big enough, the facts do not matter." Your persistence and determination will always give you the courage to keep going. Les Brown said, "Lions are fearless and cunning when they don't give up." Humanity must operate on the same principle of hunger to achieve greatness. We must have the same appetite for everything we wish to accomplish in life. Quitting will prevent us from knowing what life could have been like. It's important to stay determined and never give up. We must never stop believing in our dreams and ourselves. We must keep going. When the situation gets tough, we need to be more determined. Staying focused and never giving up is the key to success.

WINNERS ARE DOERS

The truth remains that we cannot achieve our purpose in life without becoming doers. No successful journey is complete with no sacrifice. It is ultimately this that distinguishes winners from losers. The winners are always looking for ways to fulfill their dreams. Even if the journey is long and challenging, they know that following their passion is the only way to live their lives to the fullest. They aren't sitting around waiting for things to change, as many people do. It is my experience that some people consistently pray to God for success, doing nothing to achieve it. They asked God to help them find a job, but they never applied for jobs or revised their resumes. Their response when asked why they did not go out to look for work was that they trusted God and had faith that they would receive a miracle that would change their lives forever. Nothing ever changed, much to their surprise. God can indeed do whatever He wants, but I know also that faith without works is dead. We need to decide for our lives. We must move forward. In life, we never stand still; it is an ever-changing and dynamic experience, and we will only live our best life when we become doers rather than wishers. Wishers understand the importance of defining their purpose in life, but they are not doing anything else to fulfill their dreams.

> **The failure to work on their dreams often leads to regrets in life.**

Wishers hoped for a better situation. Wishers recite the daily affirmations but don't follow through with them. They believe miracles will happen to them with some luck. Yes, miracles happen, but we must position ourselves to receive them. As the Bible says in the book of James, chapter 1:22, "Do not simply listen to the words, but become a doer." Here, the Bible is referring to wishers as hearers. Hearers and wishers can't climb the mountain. In the foothills, they ask those who have climbed to tell them about the view. There is fear in their hearts. While they wish to fly with the eagles, they do not wish to use their wings. "Success is not an accident," Brian Tracy said. "Failure is not an accident, either." By following successful people's habits every day, you can succeed. Successful people do not wait for miracles to happen. Consciously and deliberately, they strive to achieve their dreams.

To become a doer, you need to develop an obsession with the goals you want to achieve in life. Think of being rich as your second priority in life, after God. You need to make it your number two priority. If you want to find out more about it, you need to eat it, sleep it, drink it, breathe it, and ask everyone who will listen about it. By doing that, you are telling your subconscious mind what you want and what you are expecting from it. It is the doers who work on their dreams. Every day, they strive to reach the mountaintop because they want that experience. They want to live it, not just hear about it. Successful people understand that putting in the effort fuels their passion for life. The road to success is treacherous, but if you are persistent enough and work hard, you will succeed. When you surround yourself with doers, you'll notice they put everything else aside and focus on their dreams.

Don't wait for things to change just by hoping and wishing. Instead, create workable goals aligned with your vision. Don't be a spectator, become a doer!

> **Don't be a spectator, become a doer!**

It's important to remember that goals without action are meaningless. To make progress, break your goals into actionable steps and commit to acting every day. When you take small steps consistently, you'll eventually see progress, and that will propel you to keep going. Successful people understand that it's not just about doing the work, it's about doing it with passion and dedication. Break marathon goals into manageable steps, such as running a few kilometers per day and increasing intensity.

THE ROAD MAP TO SUCCESS

French writer Francois Voltaire compared life to a game of cards in which each player must accept the cards dealt to him. The player alone decides how to play and win those cards once they are in his or her hands. It is important for people who wish to be successful in life to adopt positive approaches that increase their chances of success. When one truly desires to win, they don't just play to pass the time, but they play with strong anticipation that they will receive whatever they want.

Without purpose, you may feel like you're just rushing from one thing to another. Without a purpose, your efforts are pointless. You are just spinning your wheels and exhausting yourself." Having the right purpose is crucial since without it, you will be off track. You cannot see the future. You will also have difficulty staying motivated and following through on what you have started. It will be difficult to set goals and measure progress without a purpose. Without a purpose, one cannot concentrate on what matters the most. Without it, you may waste time and energy on trivial matters that ultimately don't lead anywhere. Lack of direction may cause spending hours on social media rather than doing something meaningful.

Identifying one's desired purpose is one of the most important things one can do to achieve success. Getting to a life of financial freedom starts with reaching this threshold. The knowledge of what you want to do, however, will be useless if you don't know how to get there. Imagine you want to drive to New York but do not know which way to take; could you get there? It's highly unlikely. Financial freedom is no different. It is impossible to get there without the right strategy. Developing a new strategy is imperative if you want to change your life; otherwise, you will inevitably be disappointed.

Consider what you want from life for a moment. If you are like most people, you probably never think about what it will take to become financially independent. There is still time for you, I assure you. The time is right for you to begin your journey to financial success.

> **The first step in any journey is to recognize where you are.**

Having a clear understanding of your location allows you to plan the best route to your destination. The most important step after finding your purpose is to create a vision for your life. As Proctor noted, "A vision is what you do with your life." It is your strategy for fulfilling your purpose. To put

> **The vision is the road map, the footwork we must do to reach our goals.**

it another way, *the vision is the road map*, the footwork we must do to reach our goals. You cannot achieve your dreams by taking shortcuts. It is crucial that you come up with a plan that meets your needs and works for you. You must remain focused on your path and work hard with faith. There is no such thing as a free lunch in life, and it is impossible to get something for nothing. To get some, you must give some. So, before you can properly receive, you must become a giver. It is greater to give than to receive, as the Bible says. Invest your time in your dreams, and it will reward your efforts in due time.

DON'T DELAY CHANGING DIRECTION

If you find yourself on the wrong road, change direction. Although changing directions is difficult, it will lead you to greater things. Starting over is not an issue for winners because what matters is remaining in the game. If you don't play, you can't win. It is impossible to fulfill your dreams if you do not take steps toward them. You must take small steps day by day until you achieve your goal. Yes, there will be times when you won't know what to do next, but don't worry. Knowing our destination, we can walk the entire journey. Running to our purpose is unnecessary. In the race to success, it doesn't matter how fast you get there because it's a marathon, not a sprint. Take your time and don't give up. Keep believing in yourself and your dreams, and one day you will succeed. The experience is much like that of climbing a mountain. It may seem daunting at first, but if you take it one step at a time, you will eventually reach the summit. Don't worry about the speed or the time it takes, just focus on the journey and you will eventually get there.

EMBRACE THE TURTLE MINDSET

Now that you have defined your purpose and developed a solid strategy, it is time to develop a blueprint to get you there. Using a turtle's attitude as an example, how can we relate success in life to it? According to John Maxwell, "the right attitude at the beginning ensures success in the end." Turtles aren't the most attractive creatures in the world, but they finish more races than most animals. There is no emotion shown by them, and they are wise. Whenever they have a destination in mind, they walk toward it. Regardless of how fast others go, they don't care. As a result, they focus on their race and reach their destination at their own pace. The same applies to achieving greatness; you must focus on your goals and not worry about what others are saying. The great Tony Robins once said, "If you are constantly competing with others' views of success or financial freedom, you are going to fall behind and become frustrated." If you are chasing someone else's goal, you will always lose. Let nothing impede your race. Remember that you should always strive to be better than yesterday's version of yourself. Your greatest competitor should be yourself. You should run your race at your own pace. Known as one of the greatest singers of all time, Bob Marley once said, "The day you stop racing is the day you win."

> If you are chasing someone else's goal, you will always lose.

A successful person finishes the race. Don't lose confidence or quit because you can't see the finish line. Keeping moving in the right direction is all that matters. Your progress is being made every step of the way. Regardless of how you begin, there is no right or wrong way. What matters most is how you finish. The baby takes nine months to reach its full potential despite being conceived in a day. You won't become successful overnight, but you can change directions overnight. Success takes time and staying successful takes even longer. It is essential that you acknowledge you can finish your race. Whenever you think you can, you can.

CONSCIOUS AND SUBCONSCIOUS MIND

When people believe they can achieve their goal, they will do so. As humans, we operate on two levels: conscious and subconscious. Whenever our conscious and subconscious agree on something, then we will achieve it. Despite this, we must not have any doubts because whenever our subconscious mind experiences a conflict, it rejects it, and we get the opposite result. To avoid getting the wrong results, you must be cautious. Matthew 18:20 states, "Where two or three gather in my name, I am in the midst, and whatever they ask will be given." Let's take a moment to think about that. According to the Bible, we are the temple of God where God's spirit dwells. If our conscious and subconscious agree on anything, God's spirit—who is also God—will grant us whatever we ask for.

It is not wise to doubt yourself since your subconscious mind multiplies the seeds you plant. I believe this is the reason for many unanswered prayers. A person believes in something one minute, then lets logic run their thoughts and cultivate doubt. As the brother of Martha, Lazarus died, Jesus told her this. If they believe, they will see God's glory. Miracles can be achieved if they believe. In the same way, if you believe and do not doubt, your subconscious mind will multiply the seeds of positivity and you will reap a hundredfold return. The connection between your conscious and subconscious minds is the source of your true wealth. With those who have tried it and claim that it doesn't work, it's because they believed it on a conscious level and never accepted it subconsciously. Their blessing got blocked because of their disbelief on a subconscious level. Their thoughts weren't sown on fertile ground.

In Matthew 13, Jesus told a parable about a farmer who went out to sow, and he said some seeds fell on the path and birds ate them, and others fell on rocky ground; they sprang quickly because they had little soil, but when the sun came out, they withered and scorched because they had not rooted. Some seeds fell among thorns, preventing them from growing and blossoming; others fell on good soil, producing grain-some hundredfold, some sixty, and some thirty.

The seeds that were planted in good soil were the only ones that produced grain and multiplied it. Due to the lack of harmony between the seeds and the ground, all other seeds bore nothing else. Napoleon Hill states in The Law of Success that "the lack of harmony

> **Your subconscious mind will grant your request once there is no longer any conflict.**

is the first and only cause of failure." Your subconscious mind will grant your request once there is no longer any conflict.

The quality of our lives is largely determined by the way we think. Your perception of it defined success. According to Pastor Groeschel, what you do is determined by what you think about yourself. When you see yourself as successful, you will engage in a deliberate practice that shapes your future in that direction. Likewise, if you see yourself as someone incapable of achieving anything, you will act accordingly.

SUCCESS IS A MARATHON

The road to success is not a sprint, but a marathon. As with the turtle, you do not need to hurry. Taking action to realize your dreams is important, but it is equally important that you execute your plan carefully. Find out what works

> **The road to success is not a sprint, but a marathon.**

best for you and practice it until it becomes second nature to you.

Napoleon Hill said that to be wealthy, you must know the principles of success and failure. Ensure success by employing successful principles and avoiding those that are unsuccessful.

You will face a river of problems on the road to success; however, your ability to practice self-discipline is essential. When you experience setbacks or even temporary failures, your natural tendency might be to give up, but if you do, you can kiss your dream of success goodbye. Rather than following the same path, do something new and you will succeed.

With your newfound freedom, you can plan a plan for success. No matter where you are, it doesn't matter. The most important thing is to start because if you don't, you won't finish. It is only those who start the race who can cross the finish line. In the words of Les Brown, "You can walk your way to success." You must not wait for success to fall into your lap but position yourself ahead of time. Adrian Rogers, a spiritual leader and pastor, once said, "Man is a clever creature capable of doing anything he sets his mind to." Thanks to our resilience and persistence, we have accomplished things that seemed unimaginable. We live in a dynamic and ever-changing world. No man is exempt from passaging time. You should adopt a growth mindset if you are serious about changing your life. The American psychologist Carol Dweck writes that people who adopt the growth mindset philosophy do not focus on the now because they are always in a state of becoming. Their temporary defeats are opportunities for greater things in the future. They are persistent, determined, and willing to pay the price for success.

Before embarking on a journey of success, you should also consider the costs. Wishing and hoping won't get you to succeed until you are ready to pay the cost in advance and in full. As Jesus says in Luke 14:28,29, "Before you begin, count the cost. Who begins a building's construction without first calculating the cost to ensure enough funding exists? Alternatively, you might run out of money before completing the foundation, and then everyone would mock you."

Therefore, it is essential to take a step back and consider the costs associated with any endeavor before jumping in and investing your time and money. It is essential to be prepared and have a plan in place to ensure your success. Research the competition and the current market rate. Taking the time to explore the environment in which you'll be operating and the resources you have available to you can help you create a more effective plan. Finally, don't be afraid to ask for help or advice from experienced professionals. Once you have a plan in place, take the time to evaluate it and make sure it is achievable. Set realistic goals and break the plan down into smaller, manageable pieces. Regularly review your progress and adjust the plan as necessary. Work with others to ensure your plan is successful. Create a timeline and set deadlines to keep yourself motivated and on track. Celebrate your successes by staying motivated and focused on your goals.

> **Paying the full price upfront is important if you don't want to be called a quitter.**

CHAPTER 3

3. BELIEVING IS SEEING

The Bible defines faith as the evidence of things not seen and the substance of things hoped for. According to Webster's dictionary, faith is loyalty to a person or duty. The best way to achieve great things is to have everything you need to complete whatever task you have started. Developing faith allows you to keep going despite whatever difficulties you may face along the way. The feeling of faith can lead you to believe that you can achieve anything you want. I cannot overstate the importance of faith to me. As a result, I put my trust in God, knowing that He will equip me with the skills and knowledge I need to succeed. There is only one God, who is both omnipotent and omnipresent. To trust him with my decisions, with my life, and with everything in between would be the best course of action.

It was my faith that kept me on course and helped me win the prize. I learned through trial and error that getting knocked down was part of life, but how long I stayed down was purely determined by my attitude. In addition, I learned to develop a growth mindset based on the belief that where I am is not as important as where I go. When you have a big dream, instead of saying it is impossible, say, "I can do all things through Christ who strengthens me," and start making it happen. If you believe in what you are aiming to accomplish, your mind will accomplish it. Never forget that life always gives us what we deserve, not what we need. Therefore, it is important to always have faith in yourself and believe that you can achieve your goals, no matter how difficult. With hard work and dedication, you can achieve success. Have confidence and never give up. Set yourself up for success and have the courage to take risks. Nothing is impossible if you have the determination to make it happen. Even when things seem impossible, having faith in yourself and believing in your capabilities can help to keep you motivated. Life is unpredictable and you never know what's around the corner, so it's important to make the most of every opportunity that comes your way. For instance, if you're offered a job opportunity, it's wise to take it, even if it's not exactly what you had in mind. It could open up new doors for you and lead to even better opportunities down the line.

> **We reap what we sow.**

With a better understanding of faith, you can trust God with your future. Everything that once seemed impossible becomes possible when you trust God. In Matthew 19:26, Jesus says, "With God all things are possible." With God, you can become wealthy and enjoy the finest things in life. According to Wallace D. Wattles, "God desires to express Himself in you through your desire for riches.".

It is your job to express God's desire through faith. For example, David defeated Goliath with faith. 1 Samuel Chapter 17 explains that David was a lad when he defeated Goliath. Though he was no match for the giant, he won the battle by trusting in God. David's victory over Goliath was unthinkable. Saul, at the time, told him, "You cannot go against this Philistine and fight him; you are only a young man, and he has been a warrior since he was a boy." David had no chance in the eyes of everyone else. It was as if he were a dead man. David, however, had a very different perspective. Because of his faith, he visualized victory at the end. Seeing himself as the winner, he made this profound declaration: "This day the Lord will deliver you into my hands, and I will strike you down and cut off your head."

As Dr. Murphy Joseph said, "When we see things from the end, we have willed the means to the end." David filled his mind with victory and became a victorious man. Similarly, if you don't think about growth, you will think about fear, doubt, and disbelief, which won't help you succeed financially. It is essential to have faith that you can accomplish anything you set your mind to. Always remember that life's battles don't always go to the strongest or fastest. It is always the one who believes he can succeed, who wins.

Before we can achieve any achievement, belief must be present. Faith can remove limitations. If you believe you can achieve massive success, then you can. A person's will is the key to success. It all comes down to your state of mind. It is written in Matthew 17:20-21 that "there is no limit to what we can accomplish if we have faith the size of a mustard seed." A mustard seed is one of the smallest seeds and yet God says that is all we need to overcome any obstacle blocking our success. When people have faith, they are more likely to take risks and try new things, which increases their chances of success. It gives people the courage to persevere despite the odds. Faith helps people see a light at the end of the tunnel and motivates them to strive for success. Faith can offer emotional and psychological support in difficult times. It can also serve as a reminder that even amid hard times, there is always hope for a better tomorrow. As a lighthouse in the darkness, faith guides people toward safety, comfort, and hope amid uncertainty and despair. People have the courage to persevere because it offers hope and strength.

CHAPTER SUMMARY

The lessons of life are invaluable. If we learn from our experiences, they can serve us well. Those who succeed in life are aware of the negative, but their conscious focus is always on the positive. Through faith, they keep looking until they find what is good. You can develop a mindset that looks for answers, solutions, and for a better way when you have faith.

Making a radical shift from your past is essential to getting where you want to be. Napoleon Hill said faith transforms thoughts into spiritual equivalents. To be successful, a person must believe they can achieve success. Jesus said in Mark 9:23, "If you believe, then everything is possible."

Receiving requires first believing. A reward is waiting for you if you believe it. The law of cause and effect governs life. Everything has a cause for this law. Farmers who plant in the spring will

> **Life is an outstanding teacher.**

harvest in the fall. Hardworking students will pass their exams. A person who believes he can do something will eventually do it. Those who desire wealth must do what it takes to achieve it. When you are poor today and want to change your financial situation, you must develop a plan. Don't settle for less than what you want. Your situation will not change unless you change. Things won't work out as planned if you keep doing the same thing and expecting different results. Take steps such as budgeting, reducing spending, and setting goals for financial success.

> **Only those who believe in themselves will be rewarded.**

It doesn't matter how much faith a man professes if he does not perform the deeds to prove it. When faith does not come with proven works, it becomes nothing more than a mere statement. According to Napoleon Hill, "Faith is the only agency for harnessing and using the cosmic force of intelligence."

We will conclude this chapter with the simple truth that we cannot fully experience life until we live a purposeful life. A life lived with purpose will bring you a great sense of joy and a higher quality of life. The Bible says in Jeremiah 29:11, "For I know the plans I have for you... plans to prosper you and not to harm you plans to give you hope and a future." God intends for us to prosper and to have a wonderful future, but before we can tap into those wonderful blessings, we must discover our purpose. To achieve financial freedom or wealth, we need to reframe our thinking in life. One of the most amazing gifts the Lord has given us is our mind. Reasoning, learning, and thinking are all possible through the mind. In James Allen's words, "A man is what he thinks, his character being the sum of all his thoughts. Our thoughts are the most potent form of energy in existence."

CHAPTER 4

4. AS YOU THINK, SO YOU BECOME

W hat we think about determines who we are. It's really that simple. When we think positively, we are positive and reap positive results; when we think negatively, we attract negative results. I can't think negatively and reap positive results. The seeds we sow are the ones we reap. When the harvest comes, a farmer cannot plant corn and expect watermelon. Whatever he plants will bear similar fruit.

Believing you can make it possible to become. When you believe, great things happen. As James Allen said, "Any thought we allow to take root in our minds will eventually produce its own fruit." Good thoughts produce good fruit, and bad thoughts produce rotten fruit. Our thinking patterns can have a profound impact on our lives, so we must pay close attention to them. To change the direction of our lives for the better, we need to allow ourselves to be dominated by thoughts that can alter our thinking.

You might wonder how you can train your mind to always be positive when it is impossible to eliminate all negative thoughts. In my home country, Haiti, there is an old saying that says, "You cannot stop birds from flying on top of your head, but you can prevent them from nesting there."

Negative thoughts will always arise, but we must consciously choose not to let them control us. In Groeschel's view, if you want to change your life, you must stop trying and begin training. What is the difference between trying and

> **Negative thoughts will always arise, but we must consciously choose not to let them control us.**

training? He stated that "trying" is short-term effort, while "training" is building habits for lasting change. Thus, you do the things you can do today so you can do what you cannot do tomorrow. Get off the sidelines and into the game of financial freedom by training your mind to remain optimistic, positive, and strategic. By training your mind for success, you will be prepared to overcome any obstacles that may impede your success. Miguel de Cervantes said, "The man who prepares himself has already won half the battle." Things become easier with training and preparation.

It's up to you to decide. Changing the rest of your life is up to you. It's a challenging task, but you're capable of accomplishing it. You have the power to make it happen. It is written in the Bible that God created man in His image with all of His attributes. As a result, we are perfect and without blemishes. On earth, God has provided all the necessities for a fulfilling life.

We must respect and honor God's greatest creation, our minds. We must be diligent and monitor everything that enters our minds. Being intentional is one way to accomplish this. It is not enough to have a laissez-faire attitude. We must consciously remove anything that we deem useless, impure, or wrong from our minds. After removing these thoughts, we need to replace them with thoughts that will shape our character. Paul urges us to think of noble, righteous, lovely, and admirable things.

LIVE A LIFE OF INTENTIONALITY

Changing the course of our lives starts with renewing our minds. Continuing to do the same thing will not lead to different results. It is only when you realize you handle your life that you will change it. If you believe others handle your situation, it will stunt your growth. Change is possible at any time. The best way to begin is to practice strategic thinking. How does strategic thinking work? John Maxwell wrote, "Strategic thinking is the bridge that connects where you are now with where you want to be." It gives you a sense of direction today and builds your credibility for success tomorrow. By thinking strategically, you can break things down into manageable parts and focus on them more effectively. We can only realize your full potential when you realize you are the only person who can make your future happen. The more you improve yourself, the easier it will be for you to realize your dreams in the future.

Remember how you once thought and where it led you? How did you feel? What impact did your thinking pattern have on your life? In my experience, thinking strategically was not always practical. As a child, my parents raised me in a country where they considered being poor as a way to show humility to God. My environment shaped me. After I was destitute of money in 2017, I started reading self-help books, which changed my life forever. Having made that decision, I have lived a life of intentionality ever since. Regardless of my circumstances, I made a promise to myself to think positively. As I became more aware of how my thinking influences my habits, attitudes, and personality, I realized I could change my way of thinking. I also understood that everything in life happens for a reason and a commitment, and it serves me.

> **Everything in life happens for a reason and a commitment, and it serves me.**

Change is not a simple process, but you can do it. I believe God will assist you if you truly desire to change your life. He changed my life. Craig Groeschel said you haven't changed because you adjust your actions instead of changing your thinking. Before changing what you do, you must first change how you view yourself. It is much easier to make choices when you know who you are.

55 ABUNDANCE MINDSET

According to extensive research, an adult makes roughly 35,000 remotely conscious decisions every day. Some of those decisions may fail. Therefore, reducing the number of decisions that you make will help you focus on what matters. Chasing 100 goals at once is impossible. Zig Ziglar said, "You'll never catch a rabbit if you're trying to catch two."

Your life is not changed by the number of decisions you make, but by the quality of those decisions. Ultimately, success comes from deciding based on peace and truth. You must remind yourself daily that your attitude is more important than your intelligence. Paul said in Romans 12:2 "Don't conform to the pattern of this world but be transformed by the renewing of your mind." Then you will be able to test and approve God's will—his good, pleasing, and perfect will." As our minds become attuned to God's way, we develop different perspectives. It is up to us to control what enters our minds.

As Goddard states in The Wealth Mindset, our thoughts are our currency and need to be spent wisely. We should use our thoughts consciously to build, rather than tear down. Throughout our lives, we should strive to think positively and constructively. We should accept no thought that does not contribute to achieving our desires.

THE DESIRE FOR ABUNDANT LIFE

Ultimately, only you can stop yourself from becoming anything you desire. As Goddard put it eloquently, "You are free from the tyranny of second causes. The way you are directly related to whatever happens in your life. What we are shapes our lives, not what we want. Whenever we pollute our minds with worries, hate, racism, or anything else negative, that is what we will inevitably reap.

The mind is the most sensitive instrument God has ever created. Whatever you feed it, it will reproduce in greater quantities. Therefore, you have the choice to use your mind for good or bad. The results you will reap will not be disastrous if you use your thoughts for good. You must achieve excellent results because you harmonize them with God's law. Our belief in God and the truth of His words is unshakeable. Matthew 7:16 says, "We will know the tree by its fruit." Watermelon is the only fruit that can come from the watermelon plant. If you are poor and incapable of taking care of your daily needs, you may not be in harmony with God or yourself. You may live a double life in which you desire good things, but your thoughts are out of alignment with the universal laws of success. Regardless of what your mind thinks and believes, your subconscious mind will accept it and bring you to fruition. The subconscious mind is like a lump of clay. You can shape it any way you want. Therefore, you should think of pure, righteous, and praiseworthy things. According to David J. Schwartz, author of The Magic of Thinking Big, "When your subconscious mind works one-way, great things can happen." However, if the same mind works differently, it can also produce total failure. The subconscious mind will provide you with the thoughts, words, and actions needed to make your dreams come true if you focus on your desires. It is like planting a seed and expecting the plant to bloom - if you plant a healthy seed in a good environment and give it the necessary care, you will get a beautiful flower; however, if the seed is old or the environment is wrong, it will cannot germinate and grow.

POWER OF THE SUBCONSCIOUS MIND

Our desire for success is strong, but fear of failure can stop us from achieving great heights. The reason we're not where we want to be is because of the excuses we make. We tell ourselves a lot of stories about things we can't control, and it's amazing how many of them revolve around something we cannot control. The excuses we make are simply excuses for not acting. It is necessary to believe that you can achieve success. Sending coherent messages to your subconscious mind is the key to reconditioning yourself for success. So, this level of the mind is neutral. It has no ability to think or decide on its own. Any mental command you give to it will be obeyed. Life's logical sense is handled by the conscious. We entrust it with protecting our subconscious minds. It is up to your conscious mind to decide what goes into your subconscious mind. By monitoring everything we think, the conscious mind protects the subconscious mind from harm. As a result, no matter how negative or positive thoughts it lets through, the subconscious mind accepts them as true. Thinking of reasons you can't do something will lead to failure.

We must manage our thoughts in a manner that ensures we only entertain those thoughts that will lead us to our desired outcome. As David J. Schwartz pointed out that people are not measured by their size, weight, college degrees, or family backgrounds in the pursuit of success.

> **To achieve great things, you must think big.**

CHANGE YOUR STORY

We must let anything that opposes our desire go. You should reevaluate your beliefs about what you can achieve if you typically place limitations on what you can accomplish. By adjusting your narrative, you can change the story you tell yourself. Tony Robbins said, "Divorce the story of limitations and marry the story of the truth and everything changes." Jesus said in John 8:32, "When you learn the truth, you will be free. Unlocking your subconscious mind can lead to financial freedom. Even though old habits die hard, if we do not feed them, they will eventually die. To succeed in life, you must starve any doubts, fears, or worries that might hold you back. Taking the next step towards success is now your responsibility. Start by believing in yourself, and never give up. Identify the things that are preventing you from achieving your goals and take action to overcome them. Be mindful of your thoughts and reactions, and you can create a fresh path toward success. This is like a gardener weeding out undesired plants; by removing the obstacles in your way and nurturing yourself, you create the space for the good habits to take hold and grow.

THE SUBCONSCIOUS MIND IS A SUPERHERO

Even now, I am still a fan of superhero movies. Several months ago, I spent nearly 10 hours watching Supergirl on Netflix. It tells the story of a young woman who came to Earth from space to help humanity. Until one day, this young woman did not know she had superhero powers. It was at that moment when she had a breakthrough where she could achieve the impossible. She quickly mastered her gift, and she became a true superhero. In the same way, our subconscious mind plays the role of a superhero. God gave this mind to us as a gift, and it contains God's abilities. Despite its power, we rarely take advantage of this infinite intelligence for the things that make life worthwhile. It is possible to tap into the greatness of this universe with the right amount of willpower, but you must first accept it and believe it to be true.

When you believe you can move a mountain on the conscious level, but are doubtful on the subconscious level, you will not be able to move the mountain. Dr. Murphy Joseph said, "When our thoughts are constructive, harmonious, and peaceful, our subconscious responds and produces harmonious conditions, agreeable surroundings, and the best of everything."

Positive things produce positive outcomes.

In a nutshell, positive things produce positive outcomes.

James 1:6 says, "Whoever doubts is like a wave driven and blown by a strong wind." Therefore, we must believe at both levels. For our thoughts, desires, and cravings to manifest externally, both our conscious and subconscious minds must be at the same frequency. To avoid getting undesirable results, you must harmonize your belief with your subjective mind. By consistently repeating constructive thoughts, you can achieve this. Belief and success will follow! We can achieve success, wealth, and anything we want in life by following that formula. In the words of David J. Schwartz, "Belief, the "I'm positive-I can-attitude generates the power, skill, and energy necessary to achieve success." Essentially, when you believe you can do it, you will learn how to do it.

The process is straightforward. Getting things you've never had required operating on a frequency you've never heard before. It is impossible to achieve the future you deserve and desire with yesterday's thoughts. There needs to be an introduction to a new paradigm. Know the cause of your current situation is your old thoughts. Moving forward with the same thinking pattern will produce the same results. It is only through understanding your subconscious that you can escape your current situation. To replace old thoughts with new ones, you must replace old ones with new ones.

Top performers in any field learn to renew their mindsets. As a result, say nothing you aren't confident in believing, since your subconscious mind does not know when you are lying. If you lie, you will get the opposite of what you want. Your actions should back your words up.

As previously mentioned, the subconscious mind is a powerful tool, so how can you use it to your advantage? Being intentional is the first step. Second, you need to change your thinking. Become a positive thinker by eliminating negative thoughts.

There's no doubt about it: If you believe you can succeed, you will. Dr. Murphy Joseph's book, The Power of the Subconscious Mind, details how people have used their subconscious minds to heal. He stated, "Whatever people put inside the subconscious mind, they will receive on the outside." Our subconscious mind controls all functions of our body, whether we are awake or asleep. A story about Dr. Murphy Joseph himself struck me while reading this book. He was diagnosed with malignant skin cancer. Through a pastor's counsel, he developed an understanding of the subconscious mind's power. As a result, he fed his subconscious with the desire to be healed. A prayer he prayed was this: "I, and all my organs, were created by the infinite intelligence [God]. My body knows how to heal me. Every organ, tissue, muscle, and bone in my body was fashioned by its wisdom. The infinite intelligence [Jehovah] present within me is now transforming every atom of my being, making me whole. The healing is now taking place, and I thank God for it. My creative intelligence [Jehovah] works wonders within me." He prayed these words three times daily for about five minutes. He was completely healed within 90 days.

In the Bible, we find a similar story about a man named Job. The job was a righteous man who got sick because God bet Satan that Job would not betray him. Besides losing all his possessions, Job also lost his children. Despite his wife's advice, Job did not lose faith and cursed God. While Job remained faithful to God, he complained constantly. His complaints only made things worse. Eventually, Job realized he shouldn't allow the failures outside his mind to affect him. Upon realizing this, he focused on God instead of his problems. Suddenly, everything changed. Because of his perseverance, Job eventually surpassed the most challenging obstacles in his life with a winner's attitude. Because of his attitude, he changed the trajectory of his life, and he became a hero to us all.

Reaching your dreams means adopting the notion that anything good or bad that happens to you is something you caused with your own hands. One writer stated, "You might not be able to control the contour of your face, but you certainly can control its expression." You cannot control what happens to you, but you can control how you respond. To move forward, you must take responsibility and control of your situation. However, you must never complain because this will prevent you from achieving success. Are you familiar with the story of the children of Israel? A variety of miracles made their escape from Egypt possible. God parted the red sea, but they never made it to the promised land. Because of their lack of gratitude, they died in the wilderness. For the same reason, if you want to change your destiny, you must stop worrying and complaining about how unfair life has been to you. Concentrate on what you can control instead of worrying about what you cannot. You must also assume and increase your responsibility to draw up a solution. It is important to remember that what you sow in the subconscious mind will manifest in the physical world.

> **Changing your destiny requires that you stop worrying and complaining about how unfair life has been to you, or else you will never succeed.**

CHAPTER 5

5. ABUNDANCE MINDSET

King David wrote in Psalms 23:1, "The Lord is my Shepherd, and I shall not want." Can you imagine having nothing to worry about? As described in the Bible, this is what King David's life was like. Despite the rejection he received from his father and brothers, David became king. Likewise, you can have everything you desire as well. If you want money, you can have it. If you need better health, it is possible. A man's heart reflects his

> **A man's heart reflects his thoughts.**

thoughts. Think about what you want to become, and you will become it. When you change your mind, all will surround you with the wealth that you will ever need. If you believe you are poor, then you are poor, but if you believe you are rich, then you will be rich. The key to success lies within. In the words of Tony Robbins, thinking rich is the key to becoming wealthy. The subconscious mind is where it all begins. Invisible means of support are the subconscious mind and the conscious mind. You will become wealthy if you apply the principles of wealth consistently to your life. Your mind must be fully occupied with the concept of wealth as you grow into wealth consciousness. You will multiply whatever idea you add to your subjective mind. It is best to choose whatever you desire and deposit it into your subconscious mind. Your harvest will be poverty and opposite thoughts to your desired dream if you spend your entire day thinking about them.

If you lack anything, it is because you have not convinced your subconscious mind that you will always have more than enough for yourself and for others. Throughout Philippians 4:6, the Bible reminds us to "not be anxious about anything, but in every circumstance, by prayer and petition, with thanksgiving, present your requests to God." All of your requests should be brought to God. When you do this, avoid worrying in all aspects, since worrying does not change your situation, nor does it improve your life. Prayers align your conscious and subconscious minds, and God will grant your requests.

THE SUBCONSCIOUS MIND IS A THOUGHT RESERVOIR

According to the dictionary, a reservoir is a place where significant amounts of something are collected or accumulated. In the same way, your subconscious mind works. Whenever you deposit a thought into it, it multiplies it. But only the person who made the deposit can access this reservoir's reliable information. Having access to all the information you need is wonderful news on the one hand. Consider the scenario where you need to solve a serious problem. You can summon your subconscious mind to release the information you previously stored. As a result, you receive that information.

It's important to note that the subconscious mind also contains destructive thoughts waiting to be accessed. If you want to achieve success, you should only think positive thoughts. A wise man named David J. Schwartz once said, "The thoughts you deposit in your subconscious mind must be deliberate." Negative thoughts can lead to worry, frustration, and feelings of inferiority, all of which can lead to failure. Make it your priority to only deposit positive thoughts. It's like filling a jar with pebbles: if you take out the negative pebbles, and only fill the jar with positive pebbles, you'll end up with a jar full of positive energy and power.

In our subconscious minds, we receive whatever we put into them. If you choose to internalize untrue thoughts despite

> **It is impossible to have what you condemn or do not believe in.**

believing them to be untrue, you are unlikely to accomplish what you desire. It is impossible to have what you condemn or do not believe in. Seeing successful people as evil will not help you achieve success. By creating a confused neurotic mindset, you are creating a state of confusion. Whenever you are confused, your subconscious mind will send you hunches and opposite results. All superstitions you have accumulated about what you desire in life need to be wiped out of your mind. To be successful, it is important to have an open and positive mindset and to focus on what you want rather than what you don't want. This will enable you to be clear in your decision-making while maintaining healthy boundaries. By doing so, you can create an environment of success and achieve the goals you have set for yourself. For example, rather than worrying about failure, focus on the steps you need to take to reach your goal and the rewards that will come with achieving it.

> **Acceptance determines what you get in life.**

RECONDITIONING THE MINDSET

Reconditioning the mind takes time, which most people underestimate. You should not take this process lightly. Since we retreat and repeat our old habits, it takes a while before genuine changes take place. John Maxwell said, "You must pay your dues before you can succeed." You must form the habit of doing what unsuccessful people don't do. A person who worries that they cannot pay their bills needs to develop greater self-confidence, means, and abilities. Replacing negative thought patterns with positive ones requires regular practice. The new normal will take some time to establish, but it will eventually happen. It will take time for your new convictions to grow stronger and deeper than your old habits disappear. Adopting this new habit requires daily repetition. We can't start and quit with no results.

According to Robert A. Russell, we can change our thinking patterns in two ways. The first step is to eliminate negative thought patterns. Second, we must allow the new thinking concept to take root by letting it become part of our subconscious mind. We must become accustomed to this concept. For example, if we desire prosperity, we must think about it all day long. In the words of Ralph Waldo Emerson, "A man is what he thinks about all day long." Fix your thoughts on what you want. If you want to achieve this, you cannot allow any negative thoughts to enter. We must reject old-fashioned thinking. The third step is to open up channels for expressing the new thought by keeping it at the forefront of your mind. If the new thought is not harmonious with the desired thought, it will cause discord and limitations. To maximize results, action, hope, power, belief, conviction, and determination must fuel a new mindset. As the subconscious mind dwells on the new way of thinking, it will accept it as true and bring it to life. Mark 11:24 says, "We can have anything we desire if we believe that we already have it." We can have whatever we visualize. In Einstein's words, "Imagination is better than knowledge." If you wish to achieve success, then imagine yourself being a successful person. As the American author Jason Silva once wrote: "Imagination allows us to conceive of delightful future possibilities, pick the most amazing one, and pull the present forward to meet it."

Jesus, in Matthew 18:18, said, "Whatever you bind on earth will be bound in heaven, and whatever you loose on earth will be loosed in heaven." We can achieve anything we think we can, but we cannot achieve anything we think we cannot. The only limitations that exist are those that we set in our imaginations.

> **The only limitations that exist are those that we set in our imaginations.**

IMPEDIMENTS TO SUCCESSFUL PERFORMANCE

If you are worrying about money or an illness right now, I urge you to replace those thoughts with thoughts of abundance and great health. When people think they don't have what it takes to accomplish something, they always discover that they don't have the 'it' factor. Those people frequently come up with excuses for why they cannot accomplish their goals. Inflexibility is the most relentless enemy of achievement, growth, and success. People who fail in life always suffer from a mind-deadening thought disease called excusitis. These people would rather procrastinate and delay their tasks instead of getting them done. There is no willingness to aim again because they seem in love with past failures. Often, their failure to accept change as a catalyst for personal growth and success is a major obstacle to their success. For example, a person who lacks the flexibility to embrace new technologies or methods of doing things will find it difficult to succeed in a constantly evolving world.

FOUR COMMON TYPES OF EXCUSES

The Magic of Thinking Big by David Schwartz identifies four common types of excuses that people are prone to used to make others feel sorry for them, including, The I am not healthy excuse, the intelligence excuse, in which people think they are not smart enough to achieve anything meaningful in life, the age excuse, which is when they think they are too old or too young to change their lives, and finally, the bad luck excuse, which is probably the most dangerous excuse to overcome. People who practice this type of excuse frequently believe that some people are successful in life because of their good luck. They don't go places in life because of this way of thinking. In hopes of some sort of luck, they remain stationary. Their results will remain the same unless they vaccinate themselves against this thinking pattern.

THE POWER OF OUR IMAGINATION

The ability to imagine things is likely one of the best gifts humanity has ever received. It is possible to be and have anything we desire. There are no limits! As soon as we believe in something, all the forces of nature open up and make it possible. If you want to receive, you must believe.

Imagination is the beginning of everything.

The ability to use your imagination is crucial to achieving success in life. It was once someone's imagination that created everything you see today. Life doesn't happen by accident. To reap a harvest, you must plant. The first step toward achieving anything you want is to imagine yourself possessing it every time you think about it. It is important to back up this mental picture with faith. Believe that you have received whatever you ask for in prayer, and it will be yours. There must be no conflict between your desire for something and your imagination. Suppose you want to become financially independent, but you think you can't. As a result, you will fail, and it will doom you to failure. When we don't have conflict within ourselves, God answers our prayers. In Jim Rohn's words, "When an idea is combined with imagination and backed by genuine faith, we will succeed."

> **where there is a will, there is a way**

Successful people show this technique effectively. Their understanding is that where there is a will, there is a way, and they will not stop until they achieve their goals. Self-made millionaires achieved success by keeping their focus on their goals. For example, the late Steve Jobs, the co-founder of Apple Inc., used to say, "If you are working on something that you care about, you don't have to be pushed. The vision pulls you."

CHAPTER 6

6. EVERYONE HAS THE RIGHT TO WEALTH

It is possible for everyone to be wealthy. You are the only person who can prevent you from becoming rich. Therefore, there is no discrimination in wealth. As long as you follow its laws, it doesn't care about your background, ethnicity, or last name. A person who is not rich at this point in their life needs to change certain aspects of themselves and their habits to become rich. It's your past choices that have led you to where you are today. Making alternative choices is the key to getting new things.

Start by inspecting yourself. You cannot bring about the change you want until you know the truth about yourself. Knowing who you are is essential to achieving your goals. Ralph Waldo Emerson said, "We see only what we are in life." If you see yourself as poor, you will behave accordingly.

> **If you see yourself as poor, you will behave accordingly.**

In this way, you will start thinking about poverty constantly, which can undermine your ability to succeed. The fear of poverty paralyzes the imagination, from which all ideas flow. Without ideas, you cannot amass any fortune. To avoid poverty, you must either remove or accept the circumstances that lead to it. It is important to adopt a prosperous mindset to achieve success in life. As a result, the desire to accumulate wealth dominates the conscious mind. Any wealth we have in life came from our minds before it became tangible. It is therefore necessary to change yourself before any external changes can occur.

DON'T LET THE PAST IMPEDE YOUR FUTURE

Everything in your life that isn't working needs to be analyzed and turned into a profit. Successful people I know never let obstacles hold them back. As a result, they understood that every crisis represents both danger and opportunity. Identifying what didn't work and using it is their top priority. American psychologist William Marston said, "If there is one factor that makes life successful, it is the ability to gain dividends from defeat."

As Maxwell described in his book, Failing Forward, there are two kinds of learning. First, you learn from your past mistakes. Second, you gain wisdom by learning from others' mistakes. Avoiding mistakes by learning from others' is easier. No matter how you learn from every crisis, you will always find an opportunity if you take the time to do so. If you continuously avoid responsibility and don't own up to your mistakes, you will never gain wisdom. By renewing your thinking pattern and taking massive action, you can accomplish this.

If you want to change your life, you realize that the same patterns of thinking that have brought you here will not take you there. It's time for you to make a change. If you need help, ask for it, but become a better thinker because people who think positively attract opportunities. The German teacher Eckhart Tolle said, "The opportunity in every crisis will only emerge when all the facts are accepted and acknowledged." Once you accept and acknowledge the facts of the situation, you have opened the door to opportunity, which comes with freedom.

In order to change, we must first determine who we are. After that, we must plan an intended goal or aim to achieve. Goddard describes this primary aim as discovering whom you would like to be instead of who you are in secret. The first step to a successful life is to adopt a state of consciousness that harmonizes with what you desire. Goddard said, "People who have defined their chief aim must also observe their environment to ensure that they are not falling back into their old ways." You may not achieve your aim as quickly as you wish, but you need to remain faithful to it and think about it without quitting. If you want to become a doctor, for example, you must start thinking as if you already are.

You must imagine, see, and feel the reality of being a doctor. So, you have operated on the age-old law that states, "Having seen the end, you will have the means to achieve it."

To change your current life, you must detach from your current reactions. Before you can start living your new aim, you must accept it in your mind. We are creatures of habit who repeat mistakes, so this is not a straightforward task. Spend plenty of time purging your mind of all negative mindsets.

> **Before you can start living your new aim, you must accept it in your mind.**

Recently, I encountered a woman from Haiti who sought to establish her own business and alter the economic system in her area, yet she felt hindered by the harsh realities of life. As a young girl, she lived in a small town on the north side of Haiti, where people were very superstitious. Nothing natural ever happens to those people. Unseen forces always cause it. This young lady had a similar mindset. She believed that people in her neighborhood were trying to prevent her from achieving her dream. Since negative thinking had conditioned her, she had difficulty getting the cash needed to start her business. As a result, I explained to her that anything is possible as long as she thinks it's possible. It was only after she believed in herself that she could find funding and launch her business. As Dr. Murphy Joseph once said, "A seed deposited in the soil attracts everything that it needs to grow."

The idea that they cannot amount to anything has been infused into the subconscious mind of many people, like this young lady. Negative results will continue to occur unless they alter their state of consciousness. "Fear not only destroys your chances of intelligence, but it transmits these destructive vibrations to the minds of others and destroys their chances as well," Napoleon Hill wrote. Steer clear of those with negative attitudes, as their situation can become yours. Like our voices passing through a broadcasting station to a receiving station, negative thoughts pass from one person to another. Negative thoughts travel voluntarily, and neither the sender nor the receiver is aware of when they are doing so.

YOUR LIFE IS YOUR RESPONSIBILITY

It is your responsibility to live a fulfilling life. Your destiny is determined by the choices you make today. You will reap pleasant benefits when you make wise decisions. I am calling on you right now to change directions if you frequently make poor decisions and cannot stop. Aristotle once said, "We are what we repeatedly do." Your unfortunate decisions are the reason you are reaping undesirable consequences. When you make undesirable choices, they affect your family life, your business, your finances, and every aspect of your life. As a decent person who just wants to be successful, you might say that you are decent. It's not wrong to wish to be rich; however, it won't work. A strategy of hope does not work. Your habits will change your life, not your hope. To get riches, you must know and apply the laws of riches. The law of abundance will always provide for you when you sink it into your subconscious mind, regardless of what form success takes to you. The ability to decide what is best for yourself comes from acknowledging that you are the only one responsible for your future. Years ago, I met a young man whose parents wanted him to become an attorney instead of a singer. Although they debated the idea, he followed his dreams. Following someone else's dream would not bring you peace of mind or happiness. No matter how well-meaning the words of those who love you are, it is never a good idea to let others think for you. You can never achieve a dream that you don't own.

> **The best way to be successful is to avoid those who try to influence you.**

Negative influences will cause you to give up your God-given right to gain wealth. In the end, you will become mediocre and get whatever life hands you. Negative people never ask for what they want in life. This is considered wrong by them. They spent their lives hoping and wishing for things to change rather than making changes themselves. You must demand big things from life if you want big things in your future.

BEWARE OF NEGATIVE INFORMATION

A great mistake that people often make is feeding their minds with a good deal of negative information. They absorb everything they watch on the news and let that information and negativity sink so deep into their subconscious. People reap what they sow, yet they criticize and judge others. If you want to be rich, you must avoid negative influences at all costs. You need to use your conscious mind as the gatekeeper of your subconscious mind and not let any negative thinking leak through. Use your willpower to fully detect and inspect every thought because if you leave your mind open to the influence of other people, they will flood it with harmful thoughts. Learn to control your mind and feed it only thoughts that are aligned with your aim in life. Develop the right attitude about what you want in life and set yourself to get it. In the words of John Maxwell, "Your attitude and your potential go hand in hand."

A SUCCESS-ORIENTED ATTITUDE

Success in life depends on having the right attitude. Attitudes comprise feelings, thoughts, and actions. Throughout his life, Earl Nightingale referred to attitude as the magic word because of its profound significance. It is a magic word because it can bring us success or failure in life. How far we go in life depends on our attitude. It is impossible to achieve anything worthwhile in life if you believe you cannot. You will probably accomplish whatever you desire in life if you believe you can. Develop the attitude that you can, and you will do it. Thomas Jefferson says it, "Nothing on earth can stop the man with the right attitude from achieving his goals; nothing on earth can help the man with the wrong mental attitude."

Success is unavoidable once you develop the right attitude. To get the right results, you must alter your attitude. Have you ever met someone intelligent who had a negative attitude toward life? The results of such an individual will be the opposite, even though they possess the ability to achieve greatness. You can be intelligent and talented, but without a positive attitude, you won't be able to achieve your desired results. Even with the best qualifications and skills, a lack of attitude and enthusiasm will limit your ability to take advantage of opportunities.

WHAT IT TAKES TO BE A WINNER

Your attitude determines your fate in life. When you have a winning mindset, you'll be a winner. Winners can accomplish tasks that seem impossible because they believe in solutions. To achieve your life goals, you must align your thoughts, feelings, and actions with your desires. The thoughts you

> **The thoughts you think throughout the day determine the person you become.**

think throughout the day determine the person you become. So, you must see yourself as already successful in reaching your financial goals. Before you can attract success into your life, you need to act, talk, walk, and eat as if you are already successful.

In summary, no one is ready for success until they believe they can achieve it. Those who believe can and will accomplish anything they set their minds to. To believe, you must change your mindset from mere hope and wish. You can unlock your potential by believing in yourself; it enables you to act. It's like unlocking a treasure chest when you believe in yourself. You can unlock all your potential once you believe.

FEAR IS A STATE OF MIND

The lack of a successful attitude prevents most people from living up to their full potential. As a result, they rely on logic, which creates fear, and fear is the number one threat to success. When people consider changing their lives, they are often afraid because we are taught to fear all that is unfamiliar. It is important to understand that *fear is nothing more than a state of mind* if you want to achieve what others may deem impossible. To achieve your dreams, you must overcome your fear. Those who achieve great things have learned to defy logic and develop the right attitude.

Most people who change the course of their lives have always done things that others have considered illogical. It is said that if your idea doesn't make others think you are crazy, then it isn't big enough. Think big, as big thinkers always create opportunities for others. Don't set your goals too low since this won't require much effort. By thinking big, you'll expand your horizons and put yourself in a stronger position to succeed. In the words of Sam Ewing, a former baseball player: "There is nothing more embarrassing than watching someone do something that you said was impossible." Those who are successful understand the importance of thinking big.

They aim to reach the moon, hoping to land on the stars. Those who are unfortunate are logical and practical and always want to be realistic. Their inability to accomplish

> **They aim to reach the moon, hoping to land on the stars.**

anything consumed their waking thoughts. While they are unhappy with their 9-5 jobs, some are reluctant to leave because they don't think they can do something else. According to John Maxwell, "If you believe you cannot do something, it doesn't matter how hard you try, you've already lost." People often pursue dreams they think they can achieve rather than impossible goals. According to Steve Maraboli, "If you believe you can, you might. If you know you can, you will."

SUCCESS COMES AT A PRICE

There is a price for everything worth having. The price of success is the same as the price of failure. It is, however, necessary to pay the price upfront. As an example, Jesus died on the cross before he could save humanity. The key to success is doing what most people don't want to do. It is also important to adjust your attitude, which will help reshape your self-image and help you develop a more accurate view of yourself.

Knowing who you are, and what needs to change, is the key to achieving your life goals. Consider starting your own business; you must develop the attitude that you will succeed, even if you don't know the outcome. Failure is inevitable, but persistence will lead to success. What we believe is what we create. If we truly believe that we can succeed, then we will. As Dorothea Brandt said, "Act as if failure is impossible." If you are naturally negative or cynical, you need to develop a mindset that sees possibilities wherever they are. If your surroundings are pessimistic, you can begin by changing them. For example, if your colleagues are negative, try to surround yourself with people who are more optimistic and supportive of your pursuits. Switching from an old mindset to a new one is like getting a new car - you can travel farther and faster with more assurance. Take some time each day to think positively and focus on your goals. Take care of your mental health by engaging in activities that bring you joy and make you feel fulfilled. Believe in yourself and your capabilities–you can achieve great things!

> **What we believe is what we create.**

CHAPTER 7

7. TAKE ACTION

"Do not be deceived: God cannot be mocked. A man reaps what he sows." Galatians 6:7

People who have prepared their minds for financial success are more likely to achieve financial success. If you want to be successful, your mind has to be filled with success consciousness. Desire is the first step to success. It is rare for us to get the things we do not seek if we do not have a desire for them. You will find success if you desire it and seek it with everything you have. As Jesus said in Matthew 7:7, "If we seek, we shall find." You can't seek today and quit tomorrow. To succeed, you must be diligent in your search. The obsession with it needs to be as strong as if your life depended on it. Because it takes a strong desire for success to overcome the challenges that you will encounter on the journey. Eric Thomas said, "When you want to succeed as badly as you want to breathe, you'll succeed." When your desire for success is weak, you will give up. We can wish to change our current life situation, but we must translate those wishes into actions. Thomas Edison said, "Success is 10% inspiration and 90% perspiration." We can wish to change our current life situation, but we must also act on that wish.

> **The stairway to the top cannot be climbed unless we act.**

Making the most of what we know is all about how we apply it. Those who are wise follow up on what they hear while those who are foolish know and do not act. If you want to be among the winners, you must pair activities with faith. If you want to achieve your goals, you must turn your knowledge into activities.

The intensity of a person's desire determines whether they will quit or continue the journey. Success is like a race. We don't receive recognition for starting the race, but rather for finishing it. The Apostle Paul said it better in 2 Timothy 4:7: "I have fought the good fight; I have finished the race; I have kept the faith." The goal is to finish the race and gain the rewards. All this is nearly impossible without a strong desire for what you want to do. Desire isn't the only factor in success, for there are many other necessary elements to consider, such as hard work, dedication, and perseverance. Successful people often have a combination of all these qualities that help drive them through the race. In the end, however, that desire pushes us to take that final step and cross the finish line. For example, after months of hard work and dedication, a student may want to push themselves even further to get into their dream college.

BE THE DESIGNER OF YOUR FUTURE

Look around you; there are probably many people who hate their jobs. Even when they decide to go to work, they spend most of their time accessing digital content instead, wasting time. In a recent study, they found that workers spend an average of 2.5 hours per day on digital content unrelated to their jobs. They have cost their employers $15.5 billion in lost productivity because of their lack of interest in their occupation. They are average thinkers who did not understand the importance of their duties. As a result, their everyday thoughts and actions, along with their daily lives, eventually overwhelm them.

Yet, if people change their perceptions of their work, they can change their insights. "Life is what you make of it," my grandmother used to say. Therefore, if you only give average attention to anything you do, you will get average results. Failure is inevitable when you settle for average. Think big if you want to be rich. Cardone says, "Average won't lead you to a life of extraordinary circumstances."

The average worker goes to work simply to earn a living. Peace of mind, joy, and happiness are not things they pursue. As an example, I know several people who have pursued nursing careers because they think nurses are well paid. Helping people is not a priority for them. Because of job-related stress, they will eventually burn out. However, those who enjoy their work find pleasure, satisfaction, and fulfillment in it.

> **You will fail if you aim for average.**

Many of you do not know what you want to do yet. You are welcome to follow your path, but

> **If you don't know your destination, you may take the wrong route.**

keep in mind that if you don't know your destination, you may take the wrong route. You must be extremely cautious to avoid doing what average people have always done.

The Bible says in Philippians 4:6: "Don't worry about anything but pray and ask God for everything you need, always giving thanks for what you have." Repeating this verse daily will help you discover your purpose, which can come to you as a feeling, a hunch, or through a friend. The word of God is true. There is no need to worry about anything other than asking. God will generously meet all your needs. Whenever you lack clarity, ask God for guidance and He will lead you in the right direction. Proverbs 16:9, says, "Humans plan their course, but God establishes their steps." It's like asking for directions in a strange city and finding that the map you receive leads you exactly where you need to go. With God, you can trust that He will guide you with the right plan for your life.

FOLLOW YOUR DREAMS

I often hear that money simplifies everything, but happiness comes from following your passion. To get out of bed in the morning, you must do something that motivates you. According to Les Brown, "What men do for others, they leave behind; and what they do for themselves, they take with them." True happiness comes from making the world a better place, even if we aren't here to enjoy it. A famous Indian proverb says, "Blessed is the man who plants trees under whose shade he will never sit." People who have this attitude always enjoy peace, harmony, integrity, security, and happiness, which are the true things of life. Therefore, it is important to follow your dreams and strive to make the world a better place. Make contributions to society that will have a legacy and strive to leave a lasting impact on the world. Plant trees, volunteer, or donate to a cause whatever it may be, and take action to make the world a better place. Your contribution will be remembered and will leave a legacy that will benefit others.

> **Be the change you want to see in the world.**

Become the change you wish to see in the world. Get started today by taking a step towards making a positive difference. No matter how small your contribution may be, you can make a difference. It is like planting a seed: when nurtured with care, it will become larger and more meaningful than it was before.

BECOME AN EXPERT AT YOUR CRAFT

A key ingredient to massive success is becoming an expert in whatever you do. The idea that people can't earn a living doing what they love is an old myth. It is possible to become wealthy by doing what you love. However, you need specialized knowledge. In Think and Grow Rich, Napoleon Hill discusses two types of knowledge. Napoleon Hill discusses two types of knowledge: general knowledge and specialized knowledge. You can view general knowledge as mere information, which cannot help you gain wealth. Knowledge in itself cannot create wealth unless it is organized and intelligently directed through practical plans of action. This is why many college and university professors are poor

> **Be the change you want to see in the world.**

because they possess the knowledge, but never apply it. It is necessary to become an expert and a master in some field if you wish to become wealthy. Even though it sounds complicated, once you get started, it always gets easier.

If you study the record of anyone who has become wealthy, you see that they invested much time into becoming the best they could be in a specialized field. Therefore, learn as much as you can about the field you wish to enter. It is imperative that you become an expert. For example, if you want to become an accountant, read books, and attend seminars about that topic. Earning more money depends on how much knowledge you gain in your field. To succeed in any specialty, you must continuously pursue knowledge. As Sarah Caldwell once said: "Learn everything you can, anytime you can, from anyone you can, there will always come a time when you will be grateful for what you did."

> **Success means doing more than just enough to survive, so you must be determined to become the best you can be.**

To achieve peak performance in your field, you must follow your determination with hard work. Your ability to do it well and do it right is the key to success in any endeavor. People will be more likely to seek your services if you know you are an expert. And when people are passionate about what they do, they perform much better. Even if you lack the right talent, you can be successful in any business if you work hard and become an expert. Since genuine desire is the manifestation of power, doing things for money brings no real satisfaction in life. To live a happy life, you must follow your desires. Today, many people are stuck in jobs and businesses that they hate because they refuse to follow their passions. When a person follows their passion, they will always experience the true happiness that comes along with it.

Deciding based solely on money is not the best thing for you because it will cost you more than you can imagine. Jesus said in Mark 8:36, "What profit is it for a man to gain the universe, but lose his soul?" Because their wages are well above average, some people spend 30 years in jobs they dislike. Those wages cost them time with their children and spouse, as well as making a difference in their communities. If you're unsure what to do, remember you can do whatever you want. The subconscious would not suggest a dream to you if you were incapable of achieving it. When striving for success, you should never entertain the possibility of failure, and be willing to make sacrifices along the way. Last, you must be resilient when facing adversity. According to Roy T. Bennett, "Successful people have no fear of failure. But unsuccessful people do. Successful people have the resilience to face up to failure, to learn the lessons and adapt from it."

THE ART OF FINDING YOUR NICHE

Find something that you can do to create value for others and charge a reasonable price for it. There is no limit to what can be done with this process. Research the market to see what is in real demand, align your desire with what is in demand, and begin providing that service. By becoming creative, you will provide more services and earn more money. Subconscious ideas are waiting to come to your conscious mind and change your life forever. By convincing your subconscious that you deserve wealth, you can summon those ideas. The subconscious mind will naturally release ideas that can generate wealth if you think about it every day. If you can visualize it in your mind, you can achieve it. You will get what you need to succeed if you see yourself as a success. Take a moment to think about it. Poverty does not require much effort by the individual. The only thing they need to do is see themselves as people incapable of achieving worth in life, and they will get what they desire. In the same way, if you can visualize success, you can hold it in your hands. As you think, you become. Set realistic goals and visualize success to ensure success. Bob Proctor, an American author, speaker, and consultant, once said: "Thoughts become things. If you see it in your mind, you will hold it in your hand."

THE POWER OF A MASTERMIND GROUP

With a mastermind group, you can come up with workable ideas. A mastermind group is a group of two or more minds that form an alliance in harmony and cooperate for a purpose. Many of life's most impressive accomplishments have happened because of mastermind teams. Even if you are not an expert in a field, you can achieve greatness using the mastermind principle. Thomas Edison is a perfect example of this. He found success as an inventor by connecting with others with similar interests. Those who make use of the mastermind principle have a chance of achieving massive success. The right people around you make all the difference.

Surround yourself with a mastermind group for guidance to achieve your goals. If you practice the mastermind principle, your success will be inevitable. Jesus said it thus: "If two of you agree on earth as to anything they ask, my Father will do for them it in heaven." We have accumulated many great fortunes based on this belief. Despite your shortcomings, a mastermind group will help you become the best at whatever you choose to do. You are only as good as your network. Warren Buffett credits his success to the mastermind principle and the collective wisdom of his friends and advisors. It's like the old saying, "If you want to go fast, go alone. If you want to go far, go together." Having a network of people that you can rely on and learn from will help you achieve more in the long term than if you were to do it alone.

GET YOUR BUSINESS STARTED

Owning a business is one of the fastest ways to become wealthy. It is unlikely that you will become rich from working a 9-5 job unless you are highly skilled. Research suggests that a 9-5 job can slow down your progress. They have taught us since childhood the importance of education, hard work, and having a secure job, which can make owning your own business seem daunting. In the absence of overcoming this fear, many of us are forced to work in jobs that we dislike because we have no other choice. People who have achieved their greatest desires have persevered despite life's obstacles. By attacking, dominating, and focusing on the future, they stay in the present. Fear and discomfort become part of their learning process.

In the event you work 9-5 and still face financial difficulties, you need to take action. The sky is the limit in what you can accomplish. According to Jim Rohn, "For us to change, we need to make small changes, little by little, until we make the full turn." If you want to change your financial status, start your own business, while keeping your day job. Invest your spare time in business. If you are passionate about what you are doing, it will not be difficult.

Business ownership provides job security, independence, tax deductions, income, and flexibility. It can give you a sense of fulfillment and purpose, as well as the opportunity to make a difference in the lives of others. The challenge of owning a business can also be rewarding and fulfilling. You can learn leadership, problem-solving and communication skills. Ultimately, the rewards of owning a business can be tremendous. Create something from nothing and decide answering no one. According to Archibald Marwizi, "Entrepreneurship is discovering new ways of combining resources to create change in whatever area of life."

HONESTY IS THE BEST POLICY

Nowadays, people are too busy following people instead of becoming leaders in their fields, so the key to success is to avoid the crowd. Leadership requires learning what they do not know and using that knowledge. Their energy, motivation, and drive make them stand out. Through masterminding, they accumulate a substantial fortune. It is more common for people to trust leaders than followers. When people can trust you, they are more likely to connect and get services from you. Therefore, adding value to those who seek your services should be your top priority. You also need to improve three areas of your life continually to reach any level of success you desire: integrity, consistency, and competence. Above all, always put the well-being of people before profits whenever you seek success. Earl Nightingale said, "The person who wishes to be successful must practice integrity." Integrity builds trust, which is essential in any successful business. It also ensures that your decisions are based on doing what's right, not what's easy. Finally, integrity creates an environment where everyone is respected and valued. Maintaining integrity in business is like following a moral compass. It may be more difficult to take the right path, but the direction is always clear. As Roy T. Bennett once said: "Integrity is doing the right thing when nobody's watching, and doing as you say you would do."

Profit should not take precedence over service.

CREATE MULTIPLE STREAMS OF INCOME

As King Solomon noted in Ecclesiastes, one must invest in at least seven ventures, since a disaster may strike at any time. The concept of creating multiple ventures is noble for building wealth. It is also important to earn passive income. By adopting the concept of passive income, we can continue to generate cash flow. According to Bob Proctor, passive income comes from something you do once and get paid for multiple times over a certain period. The best way to earn passive income is to invest in dividend-paying stocks and real estate. An acquaintance of mine owns four rental properties and earns continual cash flow. Without doing much work, he just collects his money every month. As Andrew Carnegie said, "The wise young man or wage earner of today invests in real estate." Real estate investing can provide you with financial freedom. If you want to leave a legacy, it is the best vehicle to use. Grant Cardone once said, "If you die tomorrow, your real estate portfolio will continue to generate cash flow for your family."

Therefore, to achieve great wealth, you need to think of ways to earn passive income that require little of your time and attention. The time in the day for you to earn as much money as you want is not enough if you want to become wealthy by exchanging your time for money. The things that generate recurring income should be the focus of your efforts, and you can use your valuable time for things that will generate more income. In the words of Warren Buffett, "Either you make money in your sleep, or you die working for it." Passive income allows people to earn money while they sleep.

There are several ways to generate multi-stream income. Thanks to technology, starting businesses has become easier. Today, social marketing has become a popular business. The concept of social media marketing (SMM) involves promoting products and services through social media apps. Start-up costs for this type of venture are low to none. To get started, you don't need to know everything about the business. As Grant Cardone said, "No one wins in life by being smart, but by having the most passion for their cause." The key is to get started and learn as you go. You will become rich if you build a business that is customer service oriented. But the first thing to do is to learn about their needs and provide them with effective solutions. You should also focus on building relationships with your customers and other businesses in your industry. This will help you create a network of contacts that will be beneficial for your business in the long run. You should also consider ways to diversify your income sources. Taking advantage of new trends in the industry can open new opportunities for you. Finally, it's important to stay up to date with changes in the industry to ensure that you are always one step ahead. Staying up to date with emerging technologies like machine learning and AI can help you grow and create new products. This concept is like building a house - you need to reinforce the foundation with a variety of materials, so the house can withstand any changes in the environment. You also need to stay up to date on the latest techniques and advancements so you can take advantage of fresh developments and opportunities. Ultimately, this will help you create something more resilient and valuable over the long term.

SUCCESS IS NOT ABOUT SELFISHNESS

You can achieve success by ensuring that whatever you do benefits the entire world. The pursuit of success is not selfish. As Jesus says in Matthew 20:26, "Those who desire to become the greatest must first become servants." You must learn to serve the world before you can receive its many benefits. Wattles said, "God wants you to make the most of yourself, for yourself, and others." But you must do it for yourself before you can do it for others. Don't forget that you can't give what you don't have.

> **Don't forget that you can't give what you don't have.**

You must go forth with the ultimate purpose of blessing the world in everything you do. Thus, you need to eliminate thoughts or ideas that can harm others and embrace a philosophy that resonates with what Jesus taught his disciples in Mark 12:31: "Love your neighbor as yourself." For example, if you're trying to improve the world, you won't cheat, take advantage, or covet your neighbors' good.

You also need to remove any thoughts that suggest that there is a limited supply in this world. There is no need to worry, compete, or even be afraid because you are not trying to get something that belongs to someone else. Life is about creating what you want. For success to be long-lasting and satisfying, it must serve humanity. You can never enjoy the fruit of your labor permanently if you seek success at the expense of others. People who defrauded others have stolen millions and even billions of dollars. The most well-known is the story of Bernie Madoff, who perpetrated the world's largest Ponzi scheme, valued at $64.8 billion. Despite becoming wealthy at the expense of others, nature ultimately punished Bernie. After they caught him, the authorities imposed a 150-year prison sentence on him. His chronic kidney disease caused him to die in prison on April 14, 2021. Based on his private life, one would conclude that Bernie Madoff was unsuccessful and the poorest of the poor.

RESIST COMPETITION

The key to becoming successful and enjoying the fruits of success is to avoid a mindset of competition and embrace a philosophy of creation. More people will benefit whenever you adopt the creation concept and become rich. Mark Zuckerberg is an example of someone who became wealthy through creating something; he created Facebook. Accomplished people are content with their successes. It is impossible to keep those people from becoming rich. Creation avoids competition and allows you to stand out from the crowd. You don't need to worry about competing with others or being in a battle with someone else who wants the same thing. You can create something unique and original, and you will be the only one who has it. This makes it easier to find success, as you don't have to worry about competing with someone else. It can be much more fulfilling to create something unique. Finally, the rewards of creation can be much greater than those of competition. You don't have to worry about being better than anyone else to succeed. You just must be the best version of yourself and bring something new to the table. It's like gardening, where you don't have to worry about competing with anyone else, and you don't have to be the best gardener in the world to find success. All you must do is nurture your garden, provide the right conditions, and you can grow something wonderful and unique. The rewards of creation can be much greater than those of competition. As the famous Indian mystic Osho once said: "To be creative means to be in love with life. Be creative to make life more beautiful.

CHAPTER 8

8. FAILURE IS NOT THE END OF THE WORLD

"For though the righteous fall seven times, they rise again, but the wicked stumble when calamity strikes." Proverbs 24:16

History is filled with examples of people who failed spectacularly before becoming successful. Those people have also shaped history. We can follow their example when pursuing our dreams despite mountainous obstacles. Because of their refusal to quit when things weren't going well, their story lives on. Those who quit will never know the feeling of accomplishment that comes with success and may experience regret that can last a lifetime. College students who quit school will never know what it's like to walk across the stage to receive their diploma.

If you want to achieve greatness, you must learn how to bounce back after being knocked down. Daniel Walter states that successful people have daily habits different from unsuccessful people. They understand failure is part of the journey. They learn from their mistakes so they can achieve better results in the future. Despite the challenges of life, they maintain a persistent attitude. As long as they keep aiming, things will improve. Those people learn to trust themselves, which in turn builds their confidence to move forward. Successful people practice a few successful tasks every day, which builds their confidence even in fields they are unfamiliar with. Successful individuals have unique approaches to challenges and problems.

You shouldn't be afraid to fail if you want to go beyond your present situation. Seeing the good in every situation will strengthen your mind and character, so do everything you can to find the good in every situation. In my community, there is a story of a young man who came to the United States at 16 with no money and knowing no English. He has a higher income today than most Americans born in the country. Because he believed he could and had worthy goals, he rose to success. I have never heard of anyone pursuing a goal because they lack the skills. Students enroll in college because they know they will graduate and earn a degree. Likewise, you can become the best version of yourself if you believe in yourself. If you use your mind correctly, you will achieve whatever you desire. Your work, relationships, philosophy and belief system are the product of your thinking. It's important to remember that your thoughts shape your reality. What you believe you can do, you can do. Change your thinking, change your life. As Roy T. Bennett once wrote: "When you open your mind, you open new doors to new possibilities for yourself and new opportunities to help others."

PREPARE YOUR MIND FOR SUCCESS

When a person has a can-do attitude, he or she sees all situations as opportunities, even obstacles. In any endeavor, they understand that failure is only a state of mind. It will not be easy to overcome all the obstacles you will face, but you must condition yourself to succeed despite them all. It is important to

> **Temporary defeats are not final.**

reevaluate what happened, correct it, and keep moving forward after a temporary failure. Temporary defeats are not final. No matter what setbacks you have experienced, you must decide to fix them. Decide that no matter what, you can achieve your goals. It is this attitude that makes the impossible become possible. Your response to setbacks in life will determine whether you succeed or fail. As Carol Dweck pointed out, "People with a growth mindset accept challenges, persevere against setbacks, learn from criticism, and reach higher levels of achievement because of failing to improve." According to Damon Zahariades, "A growth mindset is crucial to producing big results and engineering success in any endeavor." It is important to recognize that failure is an essential part of the learning process and that mistakes can learn and grow. A growth mindset allows us to be open to learning and embrace challenges as opportunities for growth. For instance, instead of giving up when faced with a hard task, a person with a growth mindset will take the challenge as an opportunity to learn and develop new skills.

Embracing mistakes as an opportunity for growth is like taking a detour on a long journey. Though it may take you longer than the direct route, it is still a chance to explore unknown places and gain a new perspective. As Sarah Morgan put it: "Failure is a part of life. Success teaches you nothing, but failure teaches you resilience. It teaches you to pick yourself up and try again."

A GROWTH MINDSET IS ESSENTIAL

A growth mindset can be cultivated in three ways. Start by learning new skills. Second, when learning new skills, you need to be prepared to deal with challenges. As a third tip, keep a sense of purpose. Knowing why you want to do something increases your chances of completing it. A growth mindset gives us the confidence to embrace new ideas and skills, which are essential to success. This can lead to greater success in our lives and careers. It also allows us to become more resilient and creative in our problem-solving. Finally, it helps us to become better learners and thinkers.

BLAMING OTHERS IS NEVER A GOOD IDEA

As humans, we talk only about our victories. We are quick to brag about our accomplishments, but even quicker to blame others when things don't go as planned. Even though it is an instinct to blame, avoid playing the blame game because it will only lead to disaster. It is impossible to learn from past mistakes if you blame others for your shortcomings. It is also impossible for you to grow until you accept responsibility.

Taking responsibility leads to success. You will achieve your dreams when you apply this success principle in your life. You are not limited by anything. No matter what the reason for your misfortune is, try not to blame anyone else. Take your time to make an informed decision and use your logic to gain a clear understanding of the situation.

Avoiding full responsibility for your life will never bring you any good. Don't assume responsibility for someone else's errors. An Italian proverb states, "He who lets the goat be laid on his shoulders soon after must carry the cow." Don't pass the blame as it will place you in a mental prison. Taking responsibility for yourself and your actions will help you grow and become a better version of yourself. If you take responsibility for other people's mistakes, you are not allowing them to learn from them and it will only cause more problems in the future. Taking ownership of your life will help you become more independent. It will also help you gain a better understanding of yourself and the impact of your decisions.

Taking responsibility for yourself and your actions is like planting the seeds of a garden. You need to cultivate and care for it to reap the rewards in the future. If you take responsibility for other people's mistakes, you are only covering up the weeds and preventing them from growing. Responsible actions lead to a prosperous future. As the famous motivational speaker Les Brown once said: "If you take responsibility for yourself, you will develop a hunger to accomplish your dreams."

CHAPTER 9

9. PROVEN SUCCESS METHODS

To become rich, you must stop thinking about poverty and talking about it constantly. I am always upset when I hear my friends talk negatively about their lives. Somehow, they believe that their financial situation will never improve. Repeatedly, I've tried to change their views about life, but nothing works. The situation is getting worse by the minute. Forsaking poverty is the key to becoming rich. In Luke 9:60, Jesus said, "Let the dead bury the dead." Let those who love poverty enjoy it. Get moving forward and live a joyous, peaceful, and abundant life. Wealth will come to you if you think about it. Before you can help others become rich, you must first become rich yourself. According to Wattles, "To become rich is the noblest goal anyone can have in life since it includes everything else." This is a profound statement with many truths. As King Solomon said, money gives everything.

Take a moment to think about it. Rich people never have to worry about money. They do not have to worry about paying bills, setting up college funds for the kids, or donating to charities. There is no limit to what they can accomplish in life. Since they do not have to work for a living, they can learn new things that can enrich their lives. Almost everyone would say yes if asked whether they wanted to be rich, but most will never take the time to learn how. They remain in poverty because they are unaware that wealth awaits them. Instead of investing in themselves to become wealthy, they focus on short-term survival strategies. According to Jim Scott, "You can be rich by having more than you need or by needing less than you have."

If they want things to change for them, they need to make wealth the central focus of their thoughts. In addition, you can use proven success methods that have made other people rich in the past. It is my belief that those living in poverty could become rich if they elevated themselves at least 5% from where they are now.

There is no difference between those at the bottom of society's status pyramid and those at the top. We were all created equal. You can change your life. If you put in the work, no one can stop you. It is necessary to leave behind anything or anyone that is unproductive. Les Brown said, "If you're always fixing potholes, you'll never have time to build better roads." Make it your duty today to read all the success books you can find. The more knowledge you have about success, the easier it is to achieve. Act on what you learn. Put in the hard work and never give up. You have the power to create the life you want. As Therone Shellman once wrote: "It's not so much what you accomplish. But what's more important is how far you've come to accomplish what you have. Success is the measure of not mere achievement, but also how hard one had to work."

Knowledge provides power over your life and future, so the more you know, the more power you have. Do not shortchange yourself by believing that success is only for the rich. You can become wealthy as well. Do whatever you need to do as soon as possible because your future depends on it. Act now, otherwise, you will lose whatever you don't use.

> **Remember, knowledge properly applied is power.**

CHAPTER 10

10. THE LAW OF USE

We can find Ruth in the saying, "If you don't use it, you'll lose it." It has been proven time and time again that people who do not manage their time and mind wisely always end up with results they never desired. The mind is like a garden. If you stop tilling and weeding the soil, what happens? In the end, the garden will become overgrown and rumpled. Our minds and talents are no different. Our greatest gift, the mind that the Good Lord gave us, will soon become useless if we do not use it. As time passes, it becomes harder to do something about it. As James Allen said, "Just as a gardener cultivates his plot, keeping it free of weeds, we must cultivate our minds to improve our circumstances." Just remember that we don't always attract what we want in life, but rather what we are. We can only change our current situation if we inspire ourselves to take action.

> **Just remember that we don't attract what we want in life, but rather what we are.**

There have been many stories of people not taking advantage of what they had and regretting it later. The Bible amplifies a story in Matthew 25:14–30. When a man went on a journey, he entrusted his wealth to his servants. He gave five bags of gold to one person, two bags to another, and one bag to another. He then embarked on his journey. After receiving five bags of gold, the man immediately put his money to work and gained five more bags. The man with two bags of gold did the same and gained two more. The man who had received one bag dug a hole in the ground and hid his master's money there.

Eventually, the master of those servants returned and settled their accounts. The man who had received five bags of gold brought the other five. He replied, "Master, you entrusted me with five gold bags. I've gained five more." The master replied, "Well done, good and faithful servant!" I have put you in charge of many things now that you have been faithful with a few. Share your master's happiness!"

Also came the man with two gold bags. "Master," he said, "I have gained two more bags of gold from you." The master replied, "Well done, good and faithful servant!" I have put you in charge of many things now that you have been faithful with a few. Share your master's happiness!"

Finally, the man who had received one bag of gold then arrived. "Master," he said, "I knew you were a hard man, harvesting where you hadn't sown and gathering where you hadn't scattered seeds. Therefore, I hid your gold in the ground because I was afraid. Here's what you own."

"You wicked, lazy servant!" his master replied. You know I harvest where I have not sown and gather where I have not scattered seed? Then you should have deposited my money with the bankers so that when I returned, I would have received interest on it. Give the bag of gold to the person who has ten bags instead. Everyone who has will receive more, and they will have an abundance. Those who do not have, even what they have, will lose it. Throw that worthless servant outside, where there will be weeping and gnashing of teeth."

What a wonderful lesson!

Investing the resources they entrusted us with wisely benefits us. The parable teaches we are sinful if we do not use whatever God has given us wisely. God threw the servant who hid his talent out because of his laziness, and the parable teaches that laziness is a sin. Because he was afraid, he received this harsh treatment. Fear kept him in a place that couldn't bring him the results he desired. Avoid doing what this man did. Be wise and diligent instead. Invest and use the resources God has given you, no matter how small they may seem. Take risks, but trust God to provide. Believe that He will increase your talents and rewards if you use them wisely. This is like the saying, "You reap what you sow." If you put in the effort and invest in yourself, you will see the results, but if you do not, you will miss out on the fruits of your labor. As the famous English historian John Emerich Edward Dalberg Acton once wrote:

"A wise person does at once, what a fool does at last. Both do the same thing; only at different times."

CONTROL YOUR CIRCLE OF INFLUENCE

Associating with the right people can only help us succeed. When everyone around you is doing well financially, you will also do well. If you're struggling to make ends meet just like those around you, you need to change groups. Get to know new people who share your new philosophy. It is much easier to excel when you surround yourself with people with a growth mindset. Jim Rohn recommends two actions for anyone who realizes they have joined the wrong crowd. Start by separating yourself from anyone who is not moving in the same direction as you. Leave the group if they spend all they have, and you want to save money. You need to get rid of their influence quickly because they can push you off course. You should spend more time with cultured and successful people. The chemistry that exists within a group of people could be the catalyst that drives your success. Napoleon Hill once said, "Great ideas are born when minds agree in harmony." You should carefully consider your priorities and values, including your friends. Your time on this earth is very limited, so you should not waste it on non-important things.

You need to re-engineer your mindset and discover why you do what you do. Decide what you want in life, and then let it come to you. "Success comes from the person you become, not what you pursue." Be that person, and your life will never be the same. It won't happen overnight. It is too often that we seek big wins when we should look for small ones. As John Maxwell said, "Build something significant in small steps if you want it to be significant.". Follow that consistently, and you will make creative progress." Develop the discipline that will help you achieve your goals.

> **Do not be afraid to put yourself in situations that can force you to become something more and better than you currently are.**

No matter how much you feel like giving up, keep pushing yourself. Make sure you go the extra mile. If you want to find the pot of gold, go to the end of the rainbow. Always remember mingling with people who don't want to grow will not cause success.

It was once said that we are products of our environment, and statistics show that we earn between three and five thousand dollars less than those closely associated with us. It's scary if you're only hanging out with bums. I couldn't articulate it as well as Dr. Kimbro, an educator and bestselling author. As he said, If you're the smartest person in your group, you need a new group." What a profound statement. Consider how you might apply this statement to your life. Getting surrounded by people who drink alcohol might lead you to become an alcoholic.

As much as I don't want to sound judgmental, I know many people who don't want to achieve greatness. They spent their lives thinking about retirement and they are content with where they are. Is it wrong to think about retirement and be content? It is a great thing. As the Bible says, people should be content in every situation, but if they desire something more, they should not remain there. Successful people understand this concept. There is no such thing as a permanent thing in life, as they know. Even if we remain static, everything we see is in motion. Whether you're moving forward or going backward, you can't stand still. The mindset of someone very successful is often one of being on a mission. Whenever they think bigger, they always have a goal in mind. They understand that to reach their goals, they need to work hard and be dedicated, and they acknowledge that nothing is guaranteed. They also accept that failure is a part of the journey and use it to learn and grow. Successful people view life as an opportunity to make a difference and take action to make it happen. As Colin Powell once said: "There are no secrets to success: don't waste time looking for them. Success results from perfection, hard work, learning from failure, loyalty to those for whom you work, and persistence."

CHAPTER 11

11. MAKE THE BEST USE OF YOUR TIME

The key to success is making investments in every aspect of your life. A few years ago, Steve Harvey said that rich people do not sleep eight hours a day. That statement confused me because I slept only six hours a day, but I was unsuccessful. I began asking myself what I was doing wrong that hindered my growth. Having no answer, I studied successful people to discover what they were doing, and that I wasn't. Because of my research, I discovered successful people read everything they can get their hands on. They spent most of their time seeking new information to improve their wealth, health, and future. It is said that most successful business leaders read at least 60 books a year. And it takes consistency, not luck, to achieve success.

So, if you want to accumulate massive wealth, become very focused on learning how things work. Aside from winning the lottery, this is one way to become wealthy.

Wealth is a positive thing for

> **Wealth is a positive thing for rich people.**

rich people. When they experience temporary defeats, they embrace them, learn from them, and move forward with more caution. Rich people possess high levels of motivation and discipline. It is common for rich people to dream big and have massive goals in mind. They design their lives. They know that planning improves the future instead of wishing for a different outcome. As Cardone said, "Rich people dream big and then they figure out how to get bigger than that." Likewise, you need to recognize and emulate the consistently successful patterns of the rich. Initially, this might be uncomfortable, but you should push forward, anyway. You must practice those successful principles to be familiar with them. Modeling the successful habits of the rich is one of the key steps you can take in creating a successful life. These habits can range from how they think, manage their money, how they plan, and how they manage their time. Once you have identified these habits, you must implement them into your own life. This process takes time, but if you remain consistent, you will eventually see the benefits. It is important to remember that you will not become successful overnight, rather, it is a long-term process that requires dedication and hard work. For instance, if you decide to start budgeting your money, you must first create a budget and then track your expenses. Over time, you will see how much money you can save and how it can grow with consistent effort. As the famous American author, salesman, and motivational speaker Zig Ziglar once said: "Success is the doing, not the getting; in the trying, not the triumph. Success is a personal standard, reaching for the highest that is in us, becoming all that we can be. If we do our best, we are a success."

PRACTICE SETTING GOALS

Changing your life's trajectory is up to you, but you can't accomplish it unless you set some serious objectives. Before the age of 36, I had no written goals. Although I had the means to succeed, I did not know where I was heading. There was no consistency in my behavior. One week I wanted to be an attorney, the next week I wanted to be a stockbroker. After that, I wanted to become a police officer. As a result, I wasted a lot of time and was confused. As soon as I began studying successful people, my perspective changed. I realized I would not achieve my dreams unless I was focused, had big plans, and accepted those plans would guide me. As a result, I created goals that could achieve this. In the words of Jim Rohn, "Well-defined goals are like magnets. They pull you in their direction. The better you define them, the better you describe them, the harder you work on achieving them, and the stronger they pull."

Now let's talk about why setting goals is so important. Try to observe those who don't set goals and those who do. How does it look to you? Doing the same exercise made me realize that those who lack goal-setting discipline are misguided. They are content with what life has given them. If you don't design your future, you will live by someone else's standards. It's important to take control of your future by designing a blueprint.

It is easier to move forward with a step-by-step blueprint. Create a design without fear, worry, anxiety, or lack. It's difficult to do, but if you want better results, you must put in the effort. There is no gain without pain. Therefore, developing an attitude of never giving up is essential if you value something as if it were your very existence on the line.

> **There is no gain without pain.**

You need to set goals and objectives that are achievable and measurable. Aim high and always strive to reach them. Also, make sure that your goals are realistic and attainable. Set short-term and long-term goals to stay motivated and keep progressing. Establish a timeline for each goal and keep track of your progress so you can adjust as needed. Always celebrate small successes along the way and don't forget to reward yourself for reaching milestones. Stay positive and determined and focus on what you can control. Remember that failure is a part of the process, so don't give up. As the Nigerian author Idowu Koyenikan once said: "To dream of success is to set a goal of where you want to be; to wake up, take action, and achieve it is what genuine success is all about."

SUCCESS WAITS FOR NO ONE

Life is moving forward, regardless of whether we accept this reality. Time does not wait for anyone. Thus, you must act now before it's too late. No one can save you, so you need to wake up. Before you can achieve your dreams, you need to start, not figure out everything. Before you figure out every detail, you need to devote all your time to whatever it is you want to accomplish.

THE POWER OF NOW

You need to act today if you are unsatisfied with your life, but don't be hasty. As King Solomon said, "The plans of the diligent lead to profit as surely as haste leads to poverty." If you want to increase your value and quality, you must set goals immediately. One might wonder what goals to set. Every goal is the answer. Make a habit of writing everything you want in life. If you want to improve your parenting, jot down your goals. If you want a bigger account, write it down. If you desire to become a better Christian, jot it down. When something important crosses your mind, jot it down in a journal. Put your thoughts on paper. Create a long-term and short-term goal list.

LONG-TERM GOALS

This section gives you key insights on how to set long-term and short-term goals. While this might take some time, it's worth it. Take a piece of paper or a journal and start writing. Write your long-term goals first. Identify your goals within the next one to ten years. Write everything that comes to mind. Imagine yourself as a little child who wants everything he or she can think of. The beginning of a brilliant future might sound silly, but believe me, it's not. Write everything that comes to mind in 25 minutes. Take a break, then write for another 15 minutes. It's important to develop the habit of writing things down to feed the subconscious with information. As you write, your subconscious mind is receiving more information. Jim Rohn's book 7 Strategies for Wealth and Happiness lists six questions to ask when setting goals.

What do I want in life?

What do I want to be?

What do I want to see?

What do I want to have?

Where do I want to go?

What would I like to share?

You should be able to keep yourself busy for some time with these questions. During this exercise, I recommended that you distance yourself from people. You don't need to tell people what you're doing. Use this time to think about your long-term goals and how you can achieve them. Consider what you want out of life and what steps you can take to get there. Think about how you want to be remembered and what you want to accomplish in your lifetime. Reflect on what you have done in the past and how you can use your experiences to help you reach your goals. Plan for the steps you need to take to move forward. Take the time to set yourself up for success. This process is like mapping out a road trip. You need to consider the destination, your starting point, the route you want to take, and the stops along the way. You need to have a plan in place and be prepared to adjust it if needed. Taking the time to plan out your journey can save you time and energy in the long run.

It is always better to show people than to tell them.

If you are writing these goals down, make sure you use the present tense. Saying things in the present tense has a powerful effect. A famous writer once said, "When we affirm our goals in the present tense, we are tuning into our consciousness." Avoid writing or speaking in the future tense because this will show that you are placing your goals and wants in the future rather than in the present. In writing in the present tense, you take charge of your thoughts and bring forth only desirable outcomes.

Be specific about what you want to accomplish. You shouldn't just say you want a house. It is important to be detailed. Describe the house you want. List the number of rooms, the layout, the number of bathrooms, and even the number of doors. Provide a specific timeframe for your achievement. It is also important to note why this goal is important to you. Motives matter to God, especially in getting things. As the Bible states in James 3:4, "Even when you ask, you will not get it because your motives are wrong. You want only what will give you pleasure." We must have the right motives. The desire to gain wealth can't be driven by a desire to hurt people or destroy things.

SHORT-TERM GOALS

It is said that 80% of success in any endeavor comes from psychology and 20% from mechanics. For this reason, setting short-term goals is crucial to staying on track. Our short-term goals can take anywhere from a day to a year to achieve. We rely on them to keep us motivated. As we accomplish a short-term goal, we gain confidence that we can accomplish more.

> **Start with easy goals, then move on to harder ones. Make them short and sweet.**

It is also helpful to break down long-term goals into smaller, more actionable steps. There is a piecemeal approach to eating elephants. Write how long it will take you to reach your goal. Once you have completed those tasks, check them off your list. By doing this, you can recondition your mind to believe that you can accomplish your goals by breaking the limits you have placed on yourself. As a result, you will improve your self-esteem and see yourself as a finisher. When things get tough, you must keep pushing yourself and maintain the mindset that you will succeed.

According to Brian Tracy, anyone can achieve their goals by following these seven simple steps:

Step 1. Decide exactly what you want to accomplish. Let's say you want to marry and have children. Those goals must be specific in every detail.

Step 2. It is important to write them down. The power of written goals lies because you can see, touch, read, and change them if necessary. According to Jim Rohn, you must learn how to think on paper.

Step 3. Each goal should have a deadline.

Step 4. Make a list of everything that can help you achieve your goals.

Step 5. Put the most important goal at the top of your list.

Step 6. Act immediately, because goals without action are simply dreams.

Step 7. Each day, do something that will move you toward your goals. When you least expect it, you will develop the discipline you need to succeed.

If you get into the habit of writing your goals, imagine where your life will be. There is one thing I know for sure: you will become the best version of yourself. You will grow as your dreams grow. As soon as you improve yourself, everything else will fall into place. Now, should I remind you that writing your goals does not give you the life you desire? But a written goal shows that you are serious about changing your future, but you must remain disciplined to achieve your goals. The discipline you develop in life helps you stay resilient when everything around you tells you to give up. As Daniel Walter said, "Discipline means doing what you need to even when you don't feel like it."

THE POWER OF DISCIPLINE

As with other great principles, discipline is often talked about without any real action. Zig Ziglar, an author, and salesman, defined discipline as "the component that brings everything else together." It makes things happen. You can now understand why discipline is so important for a person with their daily activities. According to Grant Cardone, "Discipline is what you use to accomplish any activity until it becomes your normal operating procedure." People who lack discipline wander through life rather than living a focused, determined life. Remember that life gives you exactly what you give it, and you get better results when you act rather than try. You do not have to become perfect, but you must take swift action because that separates the rich from the poor. Poor people take a long time to decide, but they change them too quickly; rich people make quick decisions but act slowly.

A wealthy person develops the self-discipline to always do their best instead of trying. The target is more important to them than the problem because they are highly goal oriented. Getting the best results is their mission. If something fails, they discipline themselves to take on a much different approach until they find a viable solution. They also remove the word "try" from their vocabulary because a trying mentality can prevent them from achieving their dreams.

> **Getting the best results is their mission.**

WHAT'S NEXT?

Decide today that instead of trying, you will actually do it. You cannot become who you want to be if you constantly try to become it; you need to fully commit to anything you want to accomplish.

> **The key to success is to quit trying and simply do what you need to do.**

You should go all in. Playing it safe is not an option. Make sure you burn all bridges to prevent backtracking. Just like taking a leap of faith, you can't stop yourself midway once you decide to do it. Now is the right time to create the future you desire and become the person you were born to be. Make sure you don't fall into the trap of unsuccessful people who put things off. Decide as soon as possible. Gaining momentum and confidence requires you to act now. You will develop the courage you need to withstand any situation in you as you become more decisive. You will have doubts since you are stepping outside your comfort zone, but do not give up. Despite your fears, you must show courage and face your doubts. As Nelson Mandela once said, "Courage is not the absence of fear, but the triumph over it. The brave man is not one who doesn't feel fear, but one who overcomes it." Therefore, you need to take massive action now, despite your fears.

Rather than never starting, it is better to start and realize that it does not work. Don't wait until the conditions are right to start. Get started now and improve as you go. It is best not to over-analyze things because this might prevent you from starting anything meaningful. If you have been thinking about joining a gym, starting a business, or even writing a book, now is the time. Unless you act, you will remain in your current situation.

What you do right now will determine whether you become successful in life. People stay stagnant despite consuming motivation. People make excuses for why they don't start their business or eat healthily, but that only leads to failure. But getting rid of procrastination and becoming more disciplined will help them achieve their goals. This is like putting a rock at the top of a hill and waiting for it to roll down. Even if you don't do anything, the rock will eventually roll down, but the faster you push it, the faster it will roll down and the farther it will go. I can say the same about achieving goals; the faster you push yourself, the faster you will reach them. Procrastination is a bad habit of delaying what needs to be done.

STOP PROCRASTINATING

You must practice self-discipline every day to make it a habit. It should become part of your identity. Procrastination is a sin, did you know? James 4:17 says that "If someone knows the good, they should do, but does not do it, it is a sin for them." Stop telling yourself that you cannot do it or that you need to wait before you do it. You will not achieve your goals with this attitude. It's now, not tomorrow, because you don't know if you'll be alive tomorrow. Habits become easier with practice but fade without it. Self-discipline is no different. Dedication and effort are necessary for success. The law of diminishing effect states that if you don't practice something regularly, it will become more difficult with time and eventually become impossible. Therefore, it is important to practice self-discipline daily to achieve your goals and maintain your desired habits.

To reach your full potential, you need a system that works for you. As you work toward achieving your dreams, you need to change any habits that aren't helping. Replace any bad habits with good ones. If you want to quit smoking, avoid places where people smoke and even stores that sell cigarettes. The most important thing is to be consistent. It is impossible to measure the magnitude of doing small things repeatedly. If you want to quit, you need to be consistent.

Keep to a daily routine and believe in yourself. Whatever you do, believe that it is helping you achieve your goal. If something does not work, replace it with something else. Find new friends if your friends are preventing you from following your routine. Finding new people to like is easier than fulfilling your dreams. Keep your standards high, even when people criticize you. God sees everything, and He will give you what you deserve.

As you sow, you will reap. This is what the Bible says in Colossians 3:23-24: "Whatever you do, work at it with all your heart, not for human masters, knowing that you will receive an inheritance as a reward from the Lord." You are serving Christ. Avoid cutting corners. Be consistent in everything you do. Always put your words and actions first. Having integrity and being consistent increases your value as a person, since people know where you stand and will not compromise.

Maxwell says in Leader Shift, "Consistency builds a person's reputation.". When you deliver tremendous results time after time, you establish a reputation for always coming through. Rich people have this kind of reputation. Their consistency sets the tone for everything they do. Consistency is the key to success. The last thing you need to do is fall in love with discipline. You must integrate it into your life. Whatever goal will shape your life you choose to focus on. Taking consistent and massive action toward success will help you achieve such a goal. Kerouac said, "Great things are not accomplished by those who follow trends, fads, and popular opinion." Make sure you practice daily what you desire, whatever the season may bring, because repetition is key. In the words of Daniel Walter, "When you repeat an action repeatedly, you'll stop wasting time and energy debating whether you should do it. You'll just do it, just as you'd brush your teeth."

> **Little effort will yield little results. In due time, you will reap your desired harvest if you work hard.**

PRACTICE GRATITUDE

Some say that gratitude is the secret to wealth. Therefore, it is important for people who strive to succeed in life to observe the law of gratitude. As the Bible reminds us, we should always rejoice. Thank God for everything. Gratitude is acknowledging God's wisdom, knowledge, and ability. Wattles defined gratitude as "a natural principle that inaction and action are always equal and in the opposite direction." When we are more grateful, we receive more from God. From an earthly perspective, if your child is always grateful when you do something for him or her, you will be more likely to keep doing it. A mental attitude of gratitude draws us closer to God, from whom all blessings flow. We owe everything we have to God, such as health, strength, and the ability to fulfill our dreams.

You can change your life trajectory by practicing the law of gratitude. Creating a bridge allows you to receive things you never knew you could receive. My gratitude journal serves as a reminder that I have a lot to be thankful for. You should also keep a journal. Make it a habit to write the things you are grateful for. The vibration created by this will open the floodgates of heaven to pour unlimited blessings upon you. We should be grateful even if God does not answer our prayers. Thank Him in advance for what He is about to do for you.

Expressing gratitude and faith in God enables us to open our hearts and minds to receive the blessings he has for us. Being grateful for the blessings of life can help us find peace and joy in every situation. Gratitude is the key to unlocking the riches of God's blessings. Facing difficult situations, we can be thankful for the lessons learned and the strength to make it through. When we allow ourselves to be thankful for the little and big things in life, we can experience a greater sense of joy and peace. Gratitude brings reverence and changes our life and how we view the world.

CHAPTER 12

12. ATTITUDE TOWARD MONEY

Getting financial freedom can be challenging. The good news is that many people in our society have been able to navigate this arduous journey to succeed financially. Even if you feel stuck, you can achieve financial success. You don't have to master every aspect of life. Just focus on the fundamentals: philosophy, attitude, activity, results, and lifestyle.

In addition, you must change your money philosophy, which is your attitude and beliefs about money. The correct money philosophy can lead to financial independence. Therefore, you need to change your mindset and manage your finances so that money works for you rather than against you. Embrace a philosophy in which money does not dictate your actions.

Remember that our future is not determined by our wishes, but by the decisions we make today. The decision

> **The decision you make today prepares you for tomorrow.**

you make today prepares you for tomorrow. You can change your financial situation if you don't like it. You need to adopt new attitudes toward money and implement a proactive approach to managing it.

A SUCCESS PLAN IS ESSENTIAL

It is rare for people to plan for the future. Their only goal is to live life to the fullest and accept whatever comes their way. If you want to improve your financial situation, you must still make informed decisions about your finances.

John Maxwell once said, "Good decisions today will give you a better tomorrow."

> **"Good decisions today will give you a better tomorrow." – John Maxwell**

 Since we all have preconceived notions about money, making good financial decisions is not always easy. Therefore, I might make sense of a financial plan that seems baffling to you. There is no one-size-fits-all strategy for preparing for the future, but some strategies have proven to be more effective than others. Tony Robbins discussed the following strategies in his book Money Mastering the Game:

To achieve financial freedom, one must first learn to save more money and invest it in compound growth. Housel's book The Psychology of Money explains how little growth can have huge outcomes. With compound interest, we can turn even a small but consistent amount of savings into extraordinary results. An interest-bearing account containing $100 per month for 40 years will accumulate $241,059.58. Compound interest works wonders.

In addition, if you are not a saver, the simplest way to achieve financial success is to raise your income and invest the difference. There are endless opportunities to earn more money. Getting a new job, driving for Uber, or doing anything else as long as it is legal. The moment you discover a way to earn more, start saving for investments. If you want it to work, make those savings automatic. Make sure you pay yourself first and automate it. If you want to enlarge your savings and invest in stock and real estate, David Bach recommends automating it. Doing this doesn't require you to keep a budget or have self-discipline. Research shows that millionaires save around 20% of their paychecks through automation. Thus, a person's wealth is largely determined by their saving rate, rather than their income or investment returns. Wealth remains after you spend what you take in." Therefore, a high savings rate is necessary for building wealth.

Saving money for investment requires managing your expenses. It is possible, despite its daunting nature. Most people do not realize how easy it is to save money. As your income increases, decrease your spending. By desiring less, you can reduce your expenses. According to Grant Cardone, you must act broke. Invest every extra dollar in a savings account you cannot access. It is best to stay away from trendy groups. It is rare for people in this group to achieve financial success. The third thing you should do is invest in yourself. Increasing your value is crucial. How can you increase your market value? In Jim Rohn's words, work harder on yourself than on your career. You should also seek ways to serve others besides improving your skills. You'll earn more money if you serve more people. Invest in yourself in multiple ways - read books, take classes, network with like-minded people, and never stop learning. You never know who might help you in the future if you invest in your relationships. Success depends on taking care of your mental and physical health. Celebrate your successes and reflect on your progress. Create a plan to achieve your goals. Be persistent and never give up. Practice self-care and take breaks when necessary. Talk to someone you trust if you need help. Progress takes time, and failing is okay if you learn from it. Get enough sleep, eat healthy, exercise, and relax to enjoy yourself. Develop positive habits to stay motivated and focused. Believe in yourself and trust the process. Stay resilient and keep. Winston Churchill said, "Never, never, never give up."

Identifying your strengths and weaknesses can also help you create a plan to grow professionally. Furthering your education can make you more valuable to an employer. This, in turn, will help you get better job opportunities and higher salaries. It will also ensure that you are prepared for any challenges that you may face in the workplace. Increasing your value will make you more attractive to employers and can open you up to new opportunities. It will also provide you with the confidence to succeed. Investing in yourself in this way is like putting money into a savings account; you make deposits of knowledge, experience, and skills, and when you need to withdraw something, you will have more to draw on. Neo Shamon, a motivational speaker, once said: "Invest in yourself so others can invest in you."

> **"You can have everything in life you want if you just help enough other people get what they want."**
>
> **- Zig Ziglar**

CHAPTER 13

13. CHANGE YOUR DESTINY

What we think determines who we are. Before we can change our lives, we must change ourselves. Failure to act now could have catastrophic consequences. Failure can be a springboard for new things to grow and flourish. Never forget that those who never cannot have achieved nothing worthwhile. If you take the risks you need to, you may become the person you want to be, so do not be afraid to take them. We cannot achieve

> **Risks lead you closer to becoming the person you want to be, so don't be afraid to take them.**

success by settling for the familiar. To achieve your dreams, you must build them on your strengths and be willing to be uncomfortable. Recognize and take advantage of every excellent opportunity you have. To achieve success in life, you must take baby steps, practice consistency, know what you want, and be grateful for your successes. In addition, keep growing because if you don't, your life will be miserable regardless of how much money you have.

Have faith in yourself and believe in your abilities. You do not have to give up if you fail. Embrace risk. After learning from your mistakes, continue to push forward. Focus on the solution, not the problem, and develop a growth mindset. Decide and stick to it. Celebrate your victories along the way. Remember that taking risks and being willing to fail are the ways to succeed. Persevere and never give up. Always believe in yourself and trust the process. You have the power to achieve financial freedom.

> **The goal is never perfection; it is progress.**

The purpose of this book is to help you challenge your current situation. You don't have to stay in your current situation forever. You can change every aspect of your life if you wish. By taking the initiative and reflecting on your choices, you can become the best version of yourself.

The following quotes have been helpful to me. It would be great if they could help you as well. Wishing you the best!

Humility is making the everyday choice to credit God for your blessings and to credit others for your successes. - John Maxwell

Where our talents and the needs of the world crosse, there lies our vocation. - Aristotle

Always be yourself. - Steve McQueen

Three Rules to Success by Steve McQueen:

Rule 1: be yourself.

Rule 2: Study and work hard to improve yourself in your chosen craft

Rule 3: Having a positive mental attitude and the courage to try. In other words, dare to take a chance. Those who think he is now on top because of some miraculous luck forget the long hours of hard work that he spent in preparation for his career. Hard work is essential to any lasting success. Don't let work bug you.

To humans belong the plans of the heart, but from the Lord comes the proper answer of the tongue. Proverbs 16:1

In their hearts, humans plan their course, but the Lord establishes their steps. Proverbs 16:9.

The lot is cast into the lap, but every decision is from the Lord. Proverbs 16:33

One who has unreliable friends soon comes to ruin, but there is a friend who sticks closer than a brother. Proverbs 18:24
Laziness brings on deep sleep, and the shiftless go hungry. Proverbs 19:15

Always remember that repetition is key to success...

"You will not see the results you want today. Be patient. You've planted the right seeds. The harvest will come."

Craig Groeschel